PRAISE FOR *PROGRESS*

In an era when some politicians mistakenly think that progress is a narrow concept focused on just eight subjects, a serious exploration of this topic is long overdue. The Best of the Best series is true to its name: great thinkers and great practical wisdom, thought-provoking, engaging and useful.

**Bill Lucas, Director, Centre for Real-World Learning,
Professor of Learning, The University of Winchester**

The best thing about this book is the way we hear the different and varied voices of educational experts and the way the ideas are interpreted into actions we could put into practice in the classroom. As a teacher you can pick out an idea that intrigues you and consider how to make it work in your school: in the classroom, the staffroom or with individual pupils. Progress for pupils has been our mantra and this book makes you stand back and consider what it really means – and how to get more of it, wherever you work.

Jackie Beere, educational trainer, consultant and author

Progress offers practical ideas for teachers and leaders alike. The problem for many of us in education today is that there is more information out there for us to explore but not enough time to do so. Wallace and Kirkman help us to sift through the different ideas of some great educational thinkers around the issue of progress. I particularly liked the contributions of Geoff Petty, who talks us through proven evidence-based practice that will have a positive impact on the progress of students, and Mike Gershon, who explains why exemplar work with students is such a good thing as this can help students to think about the quality of their own work in comparison. As ever, Will Ord gets us thinking about progress at a deeper level by considering the different types of progress that exist, and the need for both teachers and students to stay mindful of this. I also loved Claire Gadsby's thoughts around classrooms being a place where confident, metacognitive pupils abound and how this culture can be achieved.

I suggest reading each writer's contribution. See which ideas resonate with you and perhaps go deeper into their work.

Andy Griffith, co-author of
Engaging Learners **and** *Teaching Backwards*

Progress is an exciting publication for busy teachers and school leaders. Just as Hattie brought together thousands of studies to show us what worked, Wallace and Kirkman have tapped the thinking of the most relevant experts and confined them to an accessible summary of what matters. From Hattie to Claxton to Nottingham and Hargreaves, their uplifting and encouraging words illuminate and develop the continuing and difficult dialogue about progress.

Shirley Clarke, author of *Outstanding Formative Assessment*

PROGRESS

PROGRESS

ISABELLA WALLACE AND LEAH KIRKMAN

Crown House Publishing Limited
www.crownhouse.co.uk

First published by

Crown House Publishing Ltd
Crown Buildings, Bancyfelin, Carmarthen, Wales, SA33 5ND, UK
www.crownhouse.co.uk

and

Crown House Publishing Company LLC
PO Box 2223, Williston, VT 05495
www.crownhousepublishing.com

British Library Cataloguing-in-Publication Data
A catalogue entry for this book is available from the British Library.

Print ISBN 978-1-78583-160-7
Mobi ISBN 978-1-78583-194-2
ePub ISBN 978-1-78583-195-9
ePDF ISBN 978-1-78583-196-6

LCCN 2016959888

Printed and bound in the UK by
Gomer Press, Llandysul, Ceredigion

PREFACE

When some of us started teaching many moons ago, our initial preparatory training and the subsequent professional development we received didn't really expose us to a wealth of educational thinkers, theorists or researchers. There were the staples – perhaps a pinch of Piaget here or a dusting of Dewey there ... But times are changing. Today – right now – we are witnessing the dawn of a very different informational landscape. Important, knowledgeable voices in education ring out from all directions. Not simply political ones, but the voices of experts and practitioners who have devoted significant time in their lives to the education of young people or examining the issues that surround it.

This is a wonderful development. But teachers are notoriously busy. Sometimes those of us working in education are *so* busy that being faced with such an array of diverse opinions and theories can feel overwhelming rather than helpful. It can be hard to see how we might apply ideas to our own schools and classrooms, our own year groups or subjects.

The purpose of the 'Best of the Best' series is to bring together – for the first time – the most influential voices in an accessible format A compendium of the most useful advice from the most celebrated educationalists. Each title in the series focuses on a different all-important theme and features a comprehensive collection of brief and accessible contributions from the most eminent names in education internationally. In these books you have it straight from the horse's mouth. But that's not all: in close liaison with those experts, we have developed practical, realistic, cross-curricular and cross-phase ways to make the most of these important insights *in the classroom*.

We've translated theory into practice for you, and every edition in the series is written for teachers, by teachers. Of course, if a particular concept takes your fancy and you have time to delve a little deeper, all of our experts have pointed you in the right direction for further reading. And all of a sudden the continuing professional development (CPD) voyage seems a little less overwhelming. Contented sigh.

To top it all off, the wonderful Teacher Development Trust has outlined a collaborative group approach for teachers to read the book together and try out the ideas, as well as providing helpful guidance to school leaders on how to set up CPD around the book's theme for maximum impact.

Have a breathtaking adventure discovering the best tips from the best people, and don't forget to look out for the other titles in the collection!

Isabella Wallace and Leah Kirkman

ACKNOWLEDGEMENTS

First, thanks to the wonderful experts who have generously contributed their wisdom, research and insight from all over the world. Not least to Professor Sue Wallace, whose advice and expertise have been invaluable in drawing ideas together.

Thank you to the Crown House team who believed in this ambitious project right from the outset, and whose brave faith never wavered!

We are also very grateful to David Weston and the Teacher Development Trust for collaborating with us to review the ideas and affix their guidance to the series.

Finally, we want to say a big thank you to the thousands of teachers we work with across the UK and beyond. Thank you for your enthusiasm, your energy and your endless interest in developing your practice.

CONTENTS

INTRODUCTION

What characterises effective teaching?

It's an age-old question which elicits a school filing cabinet full of responses. 'Assessment for learning?' some might cry. 'Differentiation?' 'Enthusiasm?' 'Innovation?' 'Subject knowledge?' The ingredients for great teaching are arguably countless. But the one thing that they all have in common, the one fundamental outcome that they are all intended to achieve, is *pupil progress*.

It stands to reason: we could be as passionate, as innovative or as knowledgeable as we like, but if our pupils aren't making good progress then these qualities become redundant. Let's not forget, either, that pupil progress can relate to more than simply academic progress. Good teaching promotes progress in attitude, behaviour, self-belief and self-reliance as well as skill and understanding.

So the issue of pupil progress is at the crux of all effective teaching and learning. As educators, we need to think about how we define it, how we measure it and, above all, how we ensure that it becomes a possibility for every learner. The expert contributors in this book each approach the topic of progress in their own individual way, from the philosophical and ethical to the pragmatic and purely practical. Their insights provide us accumulatively with a 360 degree exploration of a concept which is of central concern to our practice as professional educators.

Many of the contributors, including Mick Waters, Will Ord and David Didau, urge us to interrogate exactly what it is that we mean by 'progress'. They point out the implicit value judgements we may be making when applying the term uncritically and unthinkingly – just one more amid the hundreds of words we're required to use as part of our professional lexicon. Among the questions these experts encourage us to ask are: what does progress really mean? Who decides what constitutes progress? Who should set targets, and why? How do we measure progress? And how do we ensure that the structures and processes we put in place in our schools and classrooms do not leave any learner excluded?

Postmodernist philosophers have questioned the concept of progress in a historical context – the idea that humankind and its civilisation inevitably improves over time, moving towards some kind of ideal or perfect state. In philosophical terms, this belief in continual, linear improvement is referred to as one of the 'grand narratives' which humans have used since the Enlightenment to explain themselves and their history. David Didau questions this same idea in microcosm, echoing the postmodernists in his argument that progress in the classroom should not be thought of as linear, as a steadily advancing route of improvement aimed at some distant goal of perfection. Rather, he argues that progress is something achieved in fits and starts, and sometimes by circuitous and unlikely routes. This means, among other things, that progress can be more usefully viewed in terms of our learners' individual journeys rather than as a collective route. This is reminiscent of the work of the French philosopher, Lyotard, who makes the same general point when he tells us that the small stories (*les petits récits*) of individual achievement are of more value than mythical 'grand narratives' about collective progress.

Several of our contributors, including James Nottingham, Mick Waters and Mark Burns, make a similar point when they argue that progress is a personal measure, not a fixed absolute. Martin Robinson, too, questions what he refers to as 'the progress myth', while Pam Hook suggests that progress is most usefully expressed not as a forward-moving line but as a spiral where learning experiences are returned to and repeated, perhaps several times, at increasingly higher levels or at greater depth.

These contributors are all saying something about the *shape* of progress. Together, they are asserting that it is indeed not linear. The idea of linear progress is one that has served to encourage the concept of progress in education as a race towards a fixed finishing line, and this is a construct which is directly challenged by a number of contributors, not least by Pam Hook's image of a spiral, but also by those who argue that we should find a way of defining and measuring progress that does not involve the concept of competition between the learners themselves. James

Nottingham, Mick Waters and Claire Gadsby all suggest that progress should be learner centred rather than criterion based, and that – to paraphrase Claire Gadsby – it is only the pupil, not the teacher, who can demonstrate progress.

This assertion has significant implications for the way that many schools talk about progress. Too often discussions of progress are coupled with the notion of how it is being demonstrated. Sadly, the primary concern for many in this demonstration is a bureaucratic one, leaving the two most important stakeholders of progress in the classroom – the learner and the teacher – engaging in practices that are not oriented towards genuine progress. Many of the contributions in this book implore us to consider the real reasons that pupil progress needs to be visible, and that those reasons are not founded in school inspection or national benchmarks. To this end, Claire Gadsby suggests that pupils should be encouraged to develop the skills of metacognition – the ability to think about their own learning and intellectual processes in order to be able to recognise the progress they are making themselves, or would like to make. Mick Waters refers to the practice of assessing progress against externally fixed markers as an 'obsession' which should be challenged. James Nottingham makes the same important point: the measurement of progress should not be made by teachers against externally set markers, but by learners against their own personal best.

So, what are the arguments behind the resistance to externally set markers? The concern which is expressed most forcibly by these expert educationalists relates to the impact of externally imposed targets and labels and the self-limiting impact these may have on the learners themselves. As James Nottingham and Mark Burns point out, labels and 'scores' can limit learning, as can the assumptions made by teachers – assumptions that may be evident through their target-setting. Indeed, Robert Bjork warns us against making a supposition not only about what pupils can do but also about what they may need from us in order to do it.

Protecting learners from developing self-limiting beliefs is essential if we are to effectively support learning. Martin Robinson makes a very strong case here for the importance of encouraging pupils' hopes and beliefs and the need to use these as a starting point, rather than the imposition of what he calls 'mechanistic' targets. If either hope of success or belief in their own potential is at rock bottom, the pupil's ability to progress will be seriously impeded. Mark Burns makes a similar point, arguing that pupils' own expectations and beliefs are the key to making positive progress. Building confidence and self-belief, therefore, should be seen as central to the teacher's role and not simply as an optional 'soft skill'. Interestingly, Andy Hargreaves, in his contribution, extends this same concept to the need for mutual support between colleagues, which he refers to as giving 'uplift'. This idea of cheering colleagues on is underpinned by the same principles: the positive impact on performance and the progressive improvement to be derived from building confidence and self-belief.

Building confidence does not mean making learning easy, however, as several of the contributors point out. Robert Bjork, for example, argues that much is to be gained by challenging learners; that the effort necessary to overcome and work through difficulties and challenges in the learning process can result in a more secure grasp of what is learned as well as a longer lasting retention of it. John West-Burnham, too, suggests that practice is essential to effective progress in learning, and that the effort we demand of our learners can be directly proportionate to the success they achieve in reaching their goals.

Underlying these arguments is a wider point about allowing learners their voice, listening to them as experts on their own progress and recognising their individuality rather than resorting to time-saving, but opportunity-limiting, typecasting. We know that progress is sometimes best achieved by supporting pupils in moving out of their comfort zone and encouraging them to reach ever higher as they wrestle with difficult concepts and skills. However, Guy Claxton cautions that this should not be taken too far, since there is a fine line between challenging learners into making positive progress and 'over-stretching' them. Over-stretching, he explains, may result in learners becoming disheartened and losing their motivation for learning altogether.

This fine line, Claxton suggests, can best be recognised by the pupils themselves. It is they, he argues, who are ideally placed to identify when they have achieved mastery and are ready for a further challenge. He refers to this tipping point as the 'sweet spot' – the point at which the pupil is secure and confident in what they have learned and now needs to progress to the next step. Again, this raises another crucial question for us as teachers: who needs to identify the progress? Seeing tangible gains resulting from effort made is an important motivating factor; ensuring that our learners can see how far they have come from their relative starting points illustrates that their hard work has been fruitful. But to be able to identify progress, learners need to know what they should be aiming for. To this end, Mike Gershon urges the wider use by teachers of exemplar materials – examples of work which illustrate the content and standard which the pupils should be aspiring to as a next step in their learning.

On the other hand, those who place the teacher role as being just as central in identifying progression raise some interesting practical issues. Pam Hook reminds us that if we are to monitor our learners' progress, then we must have a clear idea of what we are looking for. What does progression look like in any one specific context? It can, of course, look quite different in a swimming lesson than in the learning of a foreign language! To answer this question we must have a system, or taxonomy, for making progress visible.

A wider theme emerging from these contributions – and an important one – is the question of progress and equity. The question here is about how we can best ensure that every pupil has the opportunity to progress as far as their potential will take them, unhindered by inequalities of family income, class, gender, culture or any other factor that might constitute a barrier to achievement. John Hattie makes a powerful argument, supported by practical examples, of how funding can be used effectively and equitably to enhance progress in learning for every pupil. This link between progress and the improvement of life chances resonates with the work of Sugata Mitra and the role that technology can play in this respect; while Sir John Jones, writing similarly about life chances, reminds us of the enormous influence that the quality of teaching can have on pupil motivation and progress.

This brings us finally to that other underlying theme: the fundamental impact on pupil progress of the methods we use to teach and to support their learning. Here, Geoff Petty points us to the invaluable resources provided by meta-research, which identify for us which are the most effective, progress-yielding teaching methods. Through meta-analyses, such as those conducted by John Hattie and the Education Endowment Foundation, we can discover what has been proven to work, based on accumulated evidence, over time, from a range of sources. The meta-research enables us to select our teaching methods in an informed and logical way, based on what has been proven to work best. As the Teacher Development Trust's guidance at the end of this book makes abundantly clear, this constantly growing bank of evidence-based approaches constitutes an important resource for teachers' continuing professional development.

Every expert in this book describes their thinking in their own distinctive voice. In addition, for each of their important insights, you will find a number of ways to practically implement the experts' ideas in your own classroom or even across your whole school. Some experts have provided their own strategies. Everything that is from the experts' own voices appears in white text on a black background.

Stuck for ways to flag up progress to the learners themselves without morphing into some kind of irksome cheerleader? Looking for ways to develop a classroom ethos which is conducive to progress? Interested in exploring the concept of progress over time or finding some effective 'progress producers'? Searching for ways to ensure that every pupil knows exactly what they need to do in order to make progress? Then read on to see what some of the greatest names in education today have to say about progress, and arm yourself with a plethora of practical strategies that will have you exploring pupil progress through a lens with the most important focal point of all: the best outcome for every student.

JOHN HATTIE is professor and director of the Melbourne Education Research Institute at the University of Melbourne. His ground-breaking book *Visible Learning* (2009) synthesised the results of more than fifteen years' research involving millions of students and represented the biggest ever collection of evidence-based research into what actually works in schools to improve learning.

CHAPTER 1

PUPIL PREMIUM – MONITORING WHAT WORKS

PROFESSOR JOHN HATTIE

Funding based on equity is a no-brainer; how to use these funds is the more difficult task. Ensuring that only high-probability pro-grammes of high impact are chosen is a great start. The Sutton Trust–Education Endow-ment Foundation Toolkit[1] is emerging as a key resource to sort the wheat from the chaff. It is helping to stop schools implementing low-probability programmes, stop the 'but we are different' mentality that pervades school inno-vation and stop the tendency to see satisfaction as the outcome. We know much about what works best and what does not, and we know that we can have high impact on all pupils.

The three keys are:

- Ensuring that there are the funds and capacity to evaluate the fidelity and quality of implementation.

- Developing programme logics so there is a common understanding of what the processes and outcomes are.

- Implementing excellent evaluation of the impact on student learning. (Note, I say learning, not achievement, as the latter can be too narrow.)

---

1 The EEF Teaching and Learning Toolkit is a summary of educational research on teaching 5–16-year-olds. It can be found at https://educationendowment-foundation.org.uk/toolkit.

Ensuring students enjoy and develop a passion for learning, such that they want to come back to school to learn, is often a more critical outcome. This means evaluating whether schools are inviting places to come to. The core notion is the evaluation of impact, which raises the three impact questions:

- What does impact mean (and is it shared)?
- What magnitude of impact are you aiming for?
- Is there equity in that all students gain at least a year's growth for a year's input?

From the evaluation of the pupil premium,[2] it seems the first part (use of funds) is being well undertaken, but more needs to be done to scale up the nature of successful implementation. This will involve building evidence about implementation in local contexts (within the Toolkit, for example) and developing a language of scalability – what success means – and quality evaluation resources.

But this is all the right debate – the debate about the politics of collaboration is much healthier than the politics of distraction. Issues about impact, developing a best practice of teaching and collaborating to make the difference are at the core of a flourishing and transforming school system. Such focus changes the debate about what is not working to what is working well, and has the highest probability of impacting pupils'

---

2 The pupil premium is additional funding for schools in England to raise the attainment of disadvantaged pupils.

lives. There is success in our schooling system, it is all around us, but do we have the courage to dependably recognise it, esteem it and scale it?

FURTHER READING

Fisher, Douglas, Frey, Nancy and Hattie, John A. C. (2016). *Visible Learning for Literacy, Grades K–12: Implementing the Practices That Work Best to Accelerate Student Learning* (Thousand Oaks, CA: Corwin).

Hattie, John A. C. (2009). *Visible Learning: A Synthesis of Over 800 Meta-Analyses Relating to Achievement* (London: Routledge).

Hattie, John A. C. (2012). *Visible Learning for Teachers*: Maximizing Impact on Achievement (Oxford: Routledge).

Hattie, John A. C. and Anderman, Eric (2013). *Handbook on Student Achievement* (New York: Routledge).

Hattie, John A. C., Masters, Deb and Birch, Kate (2016). *Visible Learning in Action: International Case Studies of Impact* (London and New York: Routledge).

Hattie, John A. C. and Yates, Gregory (2014). *Visible Learning and the Science of How We Learn* (London and New York: Routledge).

http://visiblelearningplus.com

PRACTICAL STRATEGIES

RECOGNISING, BUILDING AND ESTEEMING BEST PRACTICE IN A LOCAL CONTEXT

■ Do you know what your colleagues are doing in terms of continuing professional development (CPD)? In order to create a common understanding of process and impact we need to know what others are doing professionally. Is there anyone on your staff team with common pedagogical interests to yours? Are there any individuals or groups attending an upcoming local TeachMeet? What external courses have your colleagues attended this academic year? Have you or your colleagues read any books/articles/blogs that have been useful or thought-provoking? Develop a program logic among your colleagues to understand each other's theories of change, and agree short, medium and long term outcomes. Create a space for your staff team to share the various ways they are accessing CPD – this might be a physical display in the staffroom or an electronic resource to which all staff can contribute. Having a highly visible platform to see how your colleagues are developing professionally will get the dialogue going, whether this is being able to collaborate on a common initiative, sharing expertise and practice or even spotting someone from whom you can seek friendly professional advice.

■ Competition between schools can lead to educational establishments isolating themselves. But collaboration is invaluable. Seek out opportunities to visit other schools and discover what creative solutions they may have found for issues that your own school is facing. You could set up a shared electronic folder, website or chatroom where colleagues from neighbouring schools can exchange ideas, resources and experiences, post images or video clips and discuss innovations.

■ When making changes to our day-to-day classroom practice, it can be difficult to find hard and fast evidence that things are improving (or, as the case may be sometimes, not improving). We need to remember that making changes to our teaching is as much about training our learners as it is about altering our professional practice – our gut reaction is often to abandon a potentially effective teaching strategy if it doesn't go well the first time we try it out. Instead, commit to a 'triple cycle': try out the strategy in three different ways or in three different lessons before making your mind up about it. This will give you a chance to tweak your practice and get your learners used to doing things in a new way. Continue to look for evidence from student progressions that your practice is making the desired improvements.

■ Are you or your colleagues responsible for dropping in to classrooms to observe the impact of your teaching and learning in action? Could your school operate a 'treasure hunt' approach to this kind of observation, whereby the observer's responsibility is to seek out examples of great practice in every classroom they visit and display these 'treasures'. Consider using students as 'learning detectives' to help highlight the power of understanding and committing to learning. When lesson observation is seen as a thing to be feared, the sharing of good practice among colleagues is obviously going to be inhibited. John Hattie argues that it is 'a sin to go into another class and watch a teacher teach' but powerful to go into another class and help the teacher see the impact on their students. Focus on the impact not solely on the teaching. By helping colleagues in our own school to see peer observation as an invaluable tool for development, sharing and celebration of success, we can, on a small scale, contribute to what John Hattie refers to as 'collaborating to make the difference'.

EVALUATING IMPACT ON STUDENT LEARNING

■ How do you assess the impact of your teaching while you are actually teaching? What do you mean by 'impact'? What does 'a year's growth for a year's input' look like? Are these magnitudes of impact shared across your school? Make time in lessons to listen to your learners by encouraging questions and feedback. Circulate during independent work, monitoring levels of understanding and ascertaining where intervention might be necessary. Don't assume that your teaching is having the desired impact; instead, seek proof of understanding at appropriate intervals during the lesson by requiring every learner to show you their response to a pertinent question or relevant task. Mini whiteboards or electronic voting apps, which allow responses to be quickly shared by learners and quickly scanned by the teacher, are useful for this purpose.

GEOFF PETTY is the author of *Teaching Today* (5th edn, 2014), a best-selling teacher training text in the UK, and *Evidence-Based Teaching* (2nd edn, 2009) which summarises the extensive research on the best teaching methods, strategies and techniques. He has a reputation for explaining issues concerning learning and teaching in a down-to-earth but lively and inspiring way. His books have been translated into eight languages, including Chinese and Russian, and his ideas are used at a national level in Britain, Romania and Lithuania.

He has led more than 500 whole-day training sessions in colleges and schools, usually on the most effective teaching methods and on learning to learn.

His website, www.geoffpetty.com, has lots of free downloads and is very popular all over the world. He is @geoffreypetty on Twitter.

CHAPTER 2

IMPROVING PROGRESS BY LEARNING FROM THE BEST RESEARCH

GEOFF PETTY

How can you improve the progress made by your students? Hundreds of thousands of researchers have spent a century trying to answer that question, and they have come up with some powerful answers that you would be mad to ignore.

It would take many lifetimes to read all this research, but luckily some researchers have done this for you by publishing summaries of findings from the very best quality research. These summaries are variously called research reviews, meta-studies or best evidence syntheses. They tend to be written for researchers rather than for teachers so, as a teacher myself, I have tried to summarise the findings in a way teachers can easily understand and apply (Petty, 2009).

Many of the best methods that the researchers have found are at least twice as effective as conventional teaching, but only when the methods are used well. It takes time to learn how to use them, but there is hardly a better use of your time. Most of the methods involve the students doing more and the teacher doing less. The methods are also more interesting for both teacher and student. But how do we know which methods work best?

HOW SOME RESEARCHERS TEST TEACHING METHODS

In order to test teaching methods, students are divided between an *experimental group* which is taught with the methods being tested, and a *control group* which is taught the same material but without the method under test.

The control and experimental groups are carefully composed to be identical in their mix of ability, social background and so on. The control and experimental groups are taught for the same length of time by the same teachers, or by teachers of the same ability, and the students are tested to see which group has learned best. In study after study of this type, some methods produce much better learning (see the following figures).

NEVER MIND THE THEORY – DOES IT WORK IN PRACTICE?

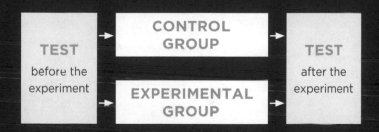

SOME METHODS ADD A GRADE
AND A HALF TO ACHIEVEMENT

Professors John Hattie and Robert Marzano have independently used careful statistical methods to average the findings of many thousands of the most rigorous studies on teaching methods and other factors that affect achievement. Their findings show that, for the best methods, if you put a student in the experimental group then, on average, they will do more than a grade and a half better than if they had been placed in the control group.

The time the teacher has to teach the topic is not a factor here. Remember that the experimental group is taught *for the same amount of time* as the control group.

The research shows that if you make the time to use these high performance teaching methods – by doing less didactic teaching, for example – then your students will do better. It may seem strange not to be able to say everything you know about the topic you are teaching, but it won't help if you do. You know too much!

Let's not confuse good explaining with good learning. The delivery of content does not guarantee its arrival. In the end, it is perhaps no surprise that students only get good at doing it – by doing it!

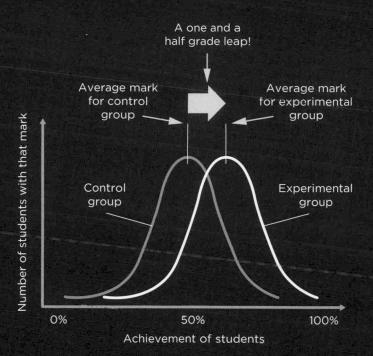

APPLYING THE BEST METHODS
WITH UNDERSTANDING

The best methods have been found to work for any subject and at any academic level, and I expect you'll guess why the methods in the practical strategies section work well: they force students to think, to make sense of what you teach and to improve their understanding. There are very many other methods that have done well in research trials (see Petty, 2009).

Just using these methods without understanding why they work will lead you to use them badly, and achievement will not be improved. We have good reason to believe that if teachers learn to use the high performance methods with understanding, students will make much more progress. This is especially true if the methods you experiment with are focused on a known weakness in students' learning or in your own teaching.

However, it will take time to learn how to use these methods well, and you will be greatly assisted if you have meetings with other teachers so you can all talk about your attempts to improve and give each other advice on what to do next. In other words, you need to do 'supported experiments', but that is another story: search online or go to http://geoffpetty.com/for-team-leaders/supported-experiments/.

FURTHER READING

Hattie, John A. C. (2009). *Visible Learning: A Synthesis of Over 800 Meta-Analyses Relating to Achievement* (London: Routledge).

Marzano, Robert J., Pickering, Debra J. and Pollock, Jane E. (2001). *Classroom Instruction That Works: Research-Based Strategies for Increasing Student Achievement* (1st edn) (Alexandria, VA: ASCD).

Mitchell, David (2008). *What Really Works in Special and Inclusive Education: Using Evidence-Based Teaching Strategies* (London: Routledge).

Petty, Geoff (2009). *Evidence-Based Teaching: A Practical Approach* (2nd edn) (Oxford: Oxford University Press).

Westwood, Peter (2003). *Commonsense Methods for Children with Special Educational Needs* (4th edn) (London: RoutledgeFalmer).

www.geoffpetty.com

PRACTICAL STRATEGIES

WHAT METHODS WORK BEST?

Let's look at some examples of methods that have done particularly well in these rigorous trials (for the detail see Petty,
2009).

■ **Same and different.** Use tasks that require the learner
to identify similarities and differences between two or
more topics or concepts, including one they are familiar
with and one they are presently studying. For example:
'Compare and contrast viral and bacterial infections.'

■ **Graphic organisers.** Ask the students to create their own
diagrammatic representation of what they are learning –
for example, in a mind-map, flow diagram or comparison
table. They move around the room to look at other
students' work to help them improve their own. Then they
self-assess their own diagram using criteria provided by
you.

■ **Decisions-decisions.** Give students a set of cards to match, group, rank or sequence. For example: 'Rank these advantages of stocktaking in order of importance, then sort them by who benefits: customer, business, supplier or investor.' Students are asked to reject your 'spurious' cards that do not describe an advantage of stocktaking.

■ **Feedback.** Give good feedback which requires that the student:

> Understands the *goals*, meaning the nature of a good piece of work. This would include understanding success criteria or assessment criteria.

> Gets a *medal* for what they have done well. This isn't a grade or mark, it is information about what aspects of the work were done satisfactorily.

> Works on a *mission*, which is a concrete way to improve their work or their next piece of work.

The teacher can provide medals, missions and goals. But there are many methods that do all this in subtle ways, such as self-assessment and peer assessment. One excellent strategy is to set students targets to address a weakness they showed in earlier work – this is called 'learning loops'.

SIR JOHN JONES is one of a small, select band of educational professionals who have not only had their achievements recognised in the New Year Honours list (2003), but have been able to help and inspire others with their knowledge and passion. One of the most entertaining, inspiring and sought-after speakers on the global educational stage, his achievements and reputation for straight-talking leadership and creativity have led him to be invited on to a number of panels and think tanks.

He served on the Labour government's Policy Action Team for Neighbourhood Renewal at the Social Exclusion Unit. He was also a member of the Headteachers' National Focus Group on Truancy and Exclusion and the Excellence in Cities Project at the Department for Education and Skills. He is currently chair of the board of Everton in the Community, a governor at the Everton Free School and Bolton St Catherine's Academy, and the chancellor of Sefton Children's University.

Sir John has written two books: *Truancy and Exclusion: A Teacher's Guide* and the best-selling *The Magic-Weaving Business* (2009), and has co-authored *Winning the H Factor: The Secrets of Happy Schools* (with Alistair Smith and Joanna Reid, London: Network Continuum Publishing, 2010).

CHAPTER 3

DEMOGRAPHICS, DESTINY AND THE MAGIC-WEAVING BUSINESS

SIR JOHN JONES

With a great deal of noise at one end and a total lack of responsibility at the other, a new baby is born in the UK every forty seconds. Its early fate will be determined by three key factors – family, income level and postcode.

For some that moment of innocence is a lottery win, for others it is the beginning of a daily struggle against the odds. Life is not fair. The literacy and emotional deficits are stark. By the age of four the child of a professional family will experience forty-five million words (Hart and Risley, 2003) and a positivity ratio of twelve encouragements to every one discouragement (Fredrickson, 2009). By comparison, on Benefits Street, though cared for as much, a child will experience only twelve million words, and for every one encouragement, two discouragements. Yet there is as much uniqueness and raw potential in one group as the other – destiny just dealt a different hand. As one in four children in the UK lives in poverty and one and a half million live in homes where no adult works (Office for National Statistics, 2015), the future appears bleak.

But the news is not all bad. There is a fourth influencing factor – the quality of teaching. After all, 'it is through education that the daughter of a peasant can become a doctor, that the son of a mineworker can become the head of the mine, that a child of farmworkers can become the president of a great nation'. Not my words – the words of Nelson Mandela (1994: 194). In a similar vein, Professor Bart McGettrick (2015) describes teaching as a 'ministry of hope'.

In the United States, a commission on 'Teaching and America's Future' explored the power of schooling to transform lives. A young woman sat before this august body. 'I was supposed to be a welfare statistic,' she explained. 'It is because of a teacher that I sit at this table. I remember her telling us one cold, miserable day that she could not make our clothing better; she could not provide us with food; she could not change the terrible segregated conditions under which we lived. She *could* introduce us to the world of reading, the world of books, and that is what she did.' Then she closed her eyes and said: 'What a world! I visited Asia and Africa. I saw magnificent sunsets; I tasted exotic foods; I fell in love and danced in wonderful halls. I ran away with escaped slaves and stood beside a teenage martyred saint. I visited lakes and streams and composed lines of verse. I knew then that I wanted to help children do the same things. I wanted to weave magic' (National Commission on Teaching and America's Future, 1996: 7).

So teachers can have a profound effect on life chances, but, sadly, not all will weave that magic. From time to time during conferences, I ask the audience to write down the names of three people who inspired them. There is always a teacher. But asked to list three people who diminished them, there is always a teacher.

In his seminal work, *Visible Learning* (2009), Professor John Hattie, describing what does and doesn't work in schools, identified teacher quality and commitment as fundamental to success. In 2011, the Sutton Trust published startling findings on the 'teacher effect'. Defining an effective teacher as one in the 84th percentile according to value-added scores and a poor teacher as one in the 16th percentile, they discovered that, taught by an effective teacher, a pupil will gain 40% more in their learning. Good teaching, it claims, has the effect of reducing class size by ten in Year 5 and by thirteen in Year 6. There is an economic boost too: teaching will add hundreds of thousands of pounds to a student's lifetime earnings. The good news is that teachers make the difference, but the bad news is that teachers make the difference.

If the quality of a country's education system cannot exceed that of its teachers (see Barber and Mourshed, 2007) and demographics are not equal to destiny, the message is clear: *teachers* do not make the difference, *great teachers* do.

FURTHER READING

Barber, Michael and Mourshed, Mona (2007). *How the World's Best Performing Education Systems Come Out On Top* (New York: McKinsey & Co.).

Fredrickson, Barbara (2009). *Positivity: Top-Notch Research Reveals the 3-to-1 Ratio That Will Change Your Life* (New York: Harmony).

Hart, Betty and Risley, Todd R. (2003). The Early Catastrophe: The 30 Million Word Gap by Age 3. *American Educator* (spring): 4–9.

Hattie, John A. C. (2009). *Visible Learning: A Synthesis of Over 800 Meta-Analyses Relating to Achievement* (London: Routledge).

Mandela, Nelson (1994). *Long Walk to Freedom: The Autobiography of Nelson Mandela* (London: Abacus).

McGettrick, Bart (2015). Speech at CHAPS National Conference, St Andrews, September.

National Commission on Teaching and America's Future (1996). *What Matters Most: Teaching for America's Future. Report of the National Commission on Teaching and America's Future* (New York: National Commission on Teaching and America's Future).

Office for National Statistics (2015). Statistical Bulletin: Working and Workless Households: 2015. Available at: http://www.ons.gov.uk/employmentandlabourmarket/ peopleinwork/employmentandemployeetypes/bulletins/ workingandworklesshouseholds/2015-10-06.

Sutton Trust (2011). Improving the Impact of Teachers on Pupil Achievement in the UK – Interim Findings (September). Available at: http://www.suttontrust.com/wp-content/uploads/2011/09/2teach-ers-impact-report-final.pdf.

PRACTICAL STRATEGIES

Sir John Jones emphasises two very important messages here: first, that it is the quality and commitment of the teacher that makes the biggest difference to pupil progress and, second, that there is a need for us to have a sound understanding of our pupils' contexts.

WEAVING MAGIC

■ Inspire your learners to reach for lofty goals by sharing with them your own learning ambition at the beginning of a term. This might be an intention to learn to play the flute, write a novel, speak Russian, spin plates and so on. Show them that your current starting point is zero or notably unskilled, and ask the pupils to offer you their advice for how you can improve. At chosen intervals over the course of the term, show the pupils how your knowledge or skill is developing and demonstrate clearly the progress you have made as a result of adhering to their original guidance. Let them celebrate this success with you. By modelling what it looks like to be an enthusiastic, committed and aspirational learner, you will be demonstrating a behaviour that has 'the power to transform lives'.

■ To inspire learners and capture their imagination in the way Sir John Jones describes, it can be helpful to consider how to *hook* learners into the subject with some personal, emotional investment. Challenge learners to consider how many degrees of separation there are between the topic they are studying and their own lives. This can be mapped in written or picture form or explored simply through discussion with another person. It can be helpful to break down the topic into a multitude of elements or branches that the learners can consider in relation to their own life experiences, their pasts and their futures. Whether it is the Second World War, Pythagoras or salsa dancing, it is always possible to uncover some kind of route connecting the topic to each learner.

■ Consider bringing in relevant inspirational speakers to talk to pupils about the topic in hand and to answer their questions. Encounters like these can create long-lasting memories that support learners' aspirational goals, thereby powering progress in the long term.

■ Are there any gaps in your learners' life experiences that you feel need filling in order for them to be in a position to fully understand and appreciate what you are teaching them? Perhaps you are making an assumption that they know what a coastline looks like, when in fact they have never visited one. Perhaps a given task relies on an understanding of how to have a civilised discussion, when in fact no one has ever modelled for them how to take turns, listen and respond or bring someone in to a conversation. If you can identify the gaps then it may be possible to go some way to plugging them. Consider how you might expose those learners to fundamental experiences they may have missed by carefully incorporating them into your programme of work. In this way, you are going some way to minimise potential barriers to progress.

MAXIMISING 'RAW POTENTIAL'

■ Boost support for pupil progress at home by involving parents as much as is possible in their child's daily learning experiences. One way to do this is to occasionally set homework tasks which require the parent to engage with their child and gain an understanding of what their child is studying. For example, try setting a task that requires the learner to explain or relate something to their parent (e.g. a poem, a mathematical process, a historical event). As part of this homework experience, the parent might then be required to fill in a pro forma to summarise and celebrate what their child has 'taught' them. While the tangible work in this case is ostensibly produced by the parent, it is in fact the pupil who has reviewed, condensed and consolidated their own understanding of the concept by 'teaching' it to someone else. At the same time, the chasm that can sometimes exist between home and school has been temporarily bridged.

■ Set up a peer-mentoring programme where older pupils can act as role models for younger ones who will benefit from observing first-hand how a committed learner behaves. The mentors might, for example, listen to their mentees read, support them with a research task or simply have regular catch-ups to hear how the mentee feels they are progressing. All relevant information can be fed back to a teacher who can, in turn, offer any further support deemed to be useful.

SUGATA MITRA is professor of educational technology at the School of Education, Communication and Language Sciences at Newcastle University.

He conducted the 'Hole in the Wall' experiment in 1999, where a computer was embedded within a wall in an Indian slum at Kalkaji, Delhi and children were allowed to use it freely. The experiment proved that kids could teach themselves computers very easily without any formal training. Sugata termed this minimally invasive education (MIE). The experiment has since been repeated in many places and has left a mark on popular culture: Indian diplomat Vikas Swarup read about Professor Mitra's experiment and was inspired to write his debut novel which went on to become the Oscar-winning movie of 2009 – *Slumdog Millionaire*.

Sugata has a PhD in physics and is credited with more than twenty-five inventions in the area of cognitive science and educational technology. He is the recipient of numerous awards from around the world, including the prestigious Dewang Mehta Award for Innovation in Information Technology in 2005 and the US$1 million TED Prize in 2013.

CHAPTER 4

SCHOOLS IN THE INTERNET AGE

SUGATA MITRA

Schools all over the world seem to pretend the Internet does not exist. Almost all school examinations do not allow the use of the Internet to answer questions. In other words, the day of the examination is possibly the only day in their life that a learner does not have access to the Internet. Two things will happen as a result:

1. Learners will increasingly want to know why they are being asked questions that can be answered in minutes using the Internet. It is like asking someone to tell the time without looking at a watch. Those who can answer questions without looking them up on the Internet will not necessarily do better in life than the ones who cannot. Indeed, many employers will be unhappy with an employee who does not use the Internet properly.

2. It will not be possible to keep the Internet out of schools and examinations. First, learners will be asked to put away their tablets and phones. Then their watches. Then their jewellery, hearing aids, glasses and, possibly, clothes. This is absurd. Internet access will become so invisible that it will no longer be possible to tell if someone is using it or not. What will happen to teaching, learning and examinations then?

Teachers and governments need to prepare to include the Internet in education. Assessment systems will need to find out if a learner can provide balanced and sensible answers to difficult questions using the Internet. Teachers will need to provide positive feedback not just for 'knowing' something, but for an ability to find answers quickly and accurately.

An ability to search for, understand and comprehend is imperative in a world where learning will happen at the point of need.

FURTHER READING

Mitra, Sugata (2012). *Beyond the Hole in the Wall: Discover the Power of Self-Organized Learning* (Kindle edn) (New York: TED Books).

PRACTICAL STRATEGIES

Sugata Mitra raises an interesting point about the importance of ensuring that pupils' progress is not impeded by schools' reluctance to embrace progress themselves. For learners to continue to make progress in life after school, it is important for schools to equip them with the skills they need to thrive in the Internet age.

PROVIDE BALANCED AND SENSIBLE ANSWERS TO DIFFICULT QUESTIONS USING THE INTERNET

As teachers, we used to think we were critical consumers of information, particularly for information retrieved from the Internet. We have an instinctive radar for trustworthy sources and we know how to sort the pertinent from the irrelevant.

Unfortunately, this impression of our critical abilities was true in a world where things changed very slowly. This is no longer the case.

Would we be able to look up the answer to the question, 'Does gravity really exist?' or 'Why do we think dark matter exists?' or 'Is DNA like a computer program?'

These are questions that are new and no books exist on them (as of July 2016). We could pretend that we know how to find these answers, but we risk misinforming the learner. There are no clear answers, but leaving these matters out is a form of denial that schools often practice. Learners will not like us for this.

■ *Do not* scaffold the task by providing a selection of specific sites to peruse that you know to be reliable, easily navigable and pitched at an appropriate level. Your judgement may be wrong or opinionated, or the sites may have changed and others come into existence by the time your class begins. Instead, use the format of Self Organised Learning Environments (SOLE). Give the learners a few Internet connections (about one connection for every four learners) and tell them that they can walk around, talk, look at others' work and change groups if they like. Ask learners to look out for information that they think may be misleading. Can they spot where opinion obscures fact, or where political or personal agendas influence perspective? Ask them to find answers to a given question, compare those answers from different Internet sources and consider the validity of each. Set assignment questions which require students to collect and evaluate evidence in order to justify a well-considered argument – for example, 'Which dictator was more tyrannical?' rather than simply 'Research both dictators'.

■ Do your students understand the basics of determining whether a website is a reliable source of information? Don't teach them, let them discover for themselves: enable them to be skilful researchers by ensuring that they can do the following:

> Identify the author of a website and discover that author's credentials.

> Ascertain the website's principal purpose.

> Determine whether a website is educational, commercial, government owned or represents a non-profit organisation.

■ Ask learners to present information in their own words or in a diagram. Tell them they can cut and paste from websites for taking notes, but they should put it all together in their own words.

■ If your question is such that it can be answered from books, you should sometimes not use the Internet and let the learners get a feel of another time. Ask them what the main differences are between researching from reading off paper as opposed to using the Internet. Remember, many of them don't know there was a world without the Internet. Since books cannot be read by more than one person, ask them how collaborative research should be done using books. Point out that books can only be passively received by one person while the Internet allows active collaboration and discussion. They need to understand that this is the engine that is driving the rapid changes we see today.

DAVID DIDAU is a teacher, speaker, trainer and writer. He is a product of social media and has no real qualification for appearing in this book beyond being opinionated about almost everything in education and having a big gob. His award-winning blog, The Learning Spy, expresses the constraints and irritations of ordinary teachers, details the successes and failures of his classroom, and synthesises his years of teaching experience through the lens of education research and cognitive psychology. As well as being read by many thousands of teachers across the world, his writing has directly influenced Ofsted and has led to him being asked to work with the UK Department for Education on reducing teachers' workload.

He has also written several books, including *The Secret of Literacy* (2014), in which he urges teachers to 'make the implicit explicit' and *What If Everything You Knew About Education Was Wrong?* (2015), which unpicks the myriad unexamined assumptions that underlie education and examines how we might realign schools with how children actually learn. His latest book, *What Every Teacher Needs To Know About Psychology* (2016), co-authored with Nick Rose, is a practical guide aimed at helping teachers understand and apply some of the most important principles of psychology in their classrooms.

CHAPTER 5

THE REAL SHAPE OF PROGRESS

DAVID DIDAU

Although we know children make progress in their knowledge and understanding of the world, we can't actually see it happen. This has hoodwinked us into believing that meaningful progress can take place in individual lessons and that learning follows a neat, linear trajectory, with children moving from knowing nothing to knowing a little, to knowing a lot, in a smooth, easily navigable and safely predictable manner. In reality, progress is more often halting, frustrating and surprising. Learning is better seen as integrative, transformative and reconstitutive – the linear metaphor in terms of movement from A to B is unhelpful. The learner doesn't *go* anywhere but develops a different relationship with what they know.

Progress is just a metaphor. It doesn't really describe objective reality; it provides a comforting fiction to conceal the absurdity of our lives. We can't help using metaphors to describe learning because we have no idea what it actually looks like. Even though our metaphors are imprecise approximations, the metaphors we use matter. They permeate our thinking. Learning is often conceived as a staircase which pupils steadily ascend. As we know from our own messy journey through life, we often seem to step backwards or sideways as often as we step up. An alternative metaphor is offered by cognitive psychologist Robert Siegler (1996), who suggests that learning is more like 'overlapping waves'. Instead of learning progressing in neat stages like a staircase, Siegler envisages learning as a gradual ebb and flow; as we encounter new rules, strategies, theories and ways of thinking, these wash through our minds like waves, sometimes obliterating what was there before, sometimes pushing suddenly forward in great surges.

This might be a more useful way to frame our thinking about progress. The image of surging and receding waves helps to explain the seemingly random retreats and swells that we experience as we grapple with new skills and tricky concepts. Slipping back is part of the liminal process of integrating new and troublesome concepts into our mental webs of understanding.

FURTHER READING

Didau, David (2012). *The Perfect Ofsted English Lesson* (Carmarthen: Independent Thinking Press).

Didau, David (2014). *The Secret of Literacy: Making the Implicit, Explicit* (Carmarthen: Independent Thinking Press).

Didau, David (2015). *What If Everything You Knew About Education Was Wrong?* (Carmarthen: Crown House Publishing).

Didau, David and Rose, Nick (2016). *What Every Teacher Needs To Know About Psychology* (Woodbridge: John Catt).

Siegler, Robert S. (1996). *Emerging Minds: The Process of Change In Children's Thinking* (New York: Oxford University Press).

PRACTICAL STRATEGIES

LEARNING AS A GRADUAL EBB AND FLOW

David Didau emphasises the importance of being aware that pupil 'performance' is not necessarily evidence of long-term learning. Knowledge and skills can sometimes be forgotten as quickly as they are amassed. Therefore, we need to ensure that there is flexibility in our teaching and our lesson planning that will allow us to respond to the ever-changing needs of our learners as they emerge. In acknowledging that our learners may well experience a 'slipping back' as a natural part of learning new things, we are also reminded that it may be necessary for the teacher to demonstrate and reinforce concepts multiple times before learners are able to effectively complete tasks independently of the teacher.

■ Being able to do something autonomously might be a sign that your learners have mastered a concept. Before you start teaching a topic, try making a list of the explicit outward signs which will indicate to you that your learners are ready to work independent of your input. Depending on what you are teaching, it may take days, weeks or even months for learners to reach this stage, but if you have identified the indicators clearly from the outset then both you and the learners will have a clear vision of their ultimate destination.

■ Celebrate and acknowledge with your learners the 'halting, frustrating and surprising' experience of making progress by modelling the process yourself. Where possible, carry out the same tasks that you set the learners and let them see you hard at work. Share your work with the pupils; discuss your choices, revelations and the setbacks you encountered. Not only will you be modelling how to 'grapple' with a difficult task, but also the act of doing so will illuminate for you the obstacles that the learners are likely to experience.

■ Allow learners to post comments on their work before they submit it to you. This gives them a personal hotline to you, enabling them to ask you questions privately, tell you the things they're struggling with or frustrated by, alert you to the parts they are most proud of and so on. Alternatively, get students to highlight where they would like feedback. Feedback which has been specifically requested is far more likely to be appreciated and acted on than unsolicited advice.

INTEGRATING NEW AND TROUBLESOME CONCEPTS

In order to remember something in the long term, we need to have thought about it. For this reason, we need to ensure that we get learners thinking about the right things in our lessons and to sustain that thinking. This means avoiding potential distractions and making sure that students are focused on the content of the subject they are learning about. Try the following strategies to encourage careful contemplation of the concept you're teaching.

- Once students are clear about the subject content, use Socratic questions that facilitate exploration and analysis of complex ideas, such as:

  > How did you reach that conclusion?

  > Is there another way of looking at this?

  > What evidence is there for this conclusion?

  > Are there any exceptions?

  > How could we disprove that?

  > What would happen if ...?

  > How does this relate to the learning?

  > Is this information sufficient?

  > Why is this important?

- Encourage learners to uncover mistakes, careless assumptions and shortfalls in their work by setting aside designated time in lessons for them to proofread their work. Proofreading is a crucial skill which forces learners to think carefully about what they have said and done.

Explicitly teach effective techniques for proofreading, such as:

> Looking for one type of problem at a time.

> Reading it aloud.

> Letting time lapse between the production and the proofreading.

> Double-checking references.

> Analysing section by section.

> Making notes about queries to check.

> Identifying repeated mistakes, etc.

■ It can be helpful to provide learners with a list of questions to help them review and think about their work in a useful way.

During his career, PROFESSOR MICK WATERS has been a teacher and head teacher as well as working at senior levels in Birmingham and Manchester local authorities. He is an Honorary Fellow of the College of Teachers and supports several educational causes. He is a patron of the Children's University, SAPERE and the Curriculum Foundation. Mick supports the National Association for Environmental Education as a vice-president and is also chair of the CoED Foundation which promotes compassionate education.

He has written books on the curriculum, teaching and learning, and leadership, as well as making presentations at numerous national and international conferences. Mick's most recent book, *Thinking Allowed On Schooling*, was published in 2013. He is passionate about the role of education in improving life chances for pupils and works with schools on raising standards and innovative approaches to learning.

CHAPTER 6

DOING WELL FOR YOUR AGE?

PROFESSOR MICK WATERS

What do Bruce Forsyth, Ken Dodd, the Queen, Doris Day, Joan Bakewell, Archbishop Desmond Tutu and the fourteenth Dalai Lama have in common? At the time of writing, they are all often described as 'doing well for their age'. It is a fascinating notion that the concept of 'doing well for your age' changes as we get older. In ageing years, being strong of limb, sharp of vision and sound of hearing are often commented upon positively, and what we mean, of course, is that the individuals are doing better than their peers. They are behind their cohort in the ageing process.

With the very young it is different. 'Doing well for your age' usually means being out in front of your cohort. Our obsession with measuring and recording individual progress has led to profiles being constructed on young children's development and the recognition that some are not as advanced as the average, which is to be expected.

Parents of young children are now told by Early Years practitioners that their child is 'slow with his phonic pick-up' or 'dropping behind with her number recognition'. Now, while it no doubt matters, finding out that your child is dropping behind can create undue worry for the parent. Here is their child, maybe just 39 months old, and the parents are being filled with concern about phonics in the same way they might worry about polio. Being a parent is hard work and worrying enough without a scorecard for your youngster being discussed at every turn.

So when does it change? At what point in life does it suddenly become alright to be behind the cohort? Do we perhaps worry too much about very young children 'being behind'?

Grandparents often despair these days about the pressure on their grandchildren. This lovely note was sent from a grandparent to a teacher:

Dear Teacher,

I understand that you are concerned about Florence's progress and that she might be getting behind with her sounds. From my observation, Florence can whisper, Florence can sing, Florence can shout, Florence can moan, Florence can laugh, argue and giggle. I don't think she has problems with sounds.

Yours sincerely,

Grandma

FURTHER READING

Claxton, Guy (2008). *What's the Point of School? Rediscovering the Heart of Education* (Oxford: Oneworld).

Claxton, Guy and Lucas, Bill (2015). *Educating Ruby: What Our Children Really Need to Learn* (Carmarthen: Crown House Publishing).

Coyle, Daniel (2010). *The Talent Code: Greatness Isn't Born. It's Grown* (New York: Arrow).

Dweck, Carol (2008). *Mindset: The New Psychology of Success* (New York: Ballantine Books).

Griffith, Andy and Burns, Mark (2014). *Teaching Backwards: Outstanding Teaching* (Carmarthen: Crown House Publishing).

Waters, Mick (2013). *Thinking Allowed On Schooling* (Carmarthen: Independent Thinking Press).

PRACTICAL STRATEGIES

DOING WELL FOR YOUR AGE VS. DOING WELL FOR YOURSELF

Mick Waters' empathy for parental concerns about progress relative to the 'average' is an inspired perspective. We get so caught up in our data, and ensuring that it reflects well on our schools and our teaching, that it is easy to become overly objective when reporting performance. Accurately reporting learners' progress to parents in relation to data-generated targets is vital, but does comparison to the 'average' need to be the dominant driving force?

Ipsative assessment is an interesting paradigm shift to consider when framing discussions about progress with parents. The thrust of ipsative assessment is the notion of beating your 'personal best' and using targeted feedback to close identified gaps so that you can continue to improve relative to your own performance. In terms of discussions with parents, this slight shift from talking about performance against a national standard, or even the standard of the cohort their child is in, to one that is personalised to their child has the potential to reduce the neurosis that can come from perceiving your child as being behind the norm. Focusing the feedback on ways to move on in relation to the child's own personal targets is also the best way to enable parents to support their child's progress.

Try the following to help improve home–school communication about pupils' 'personal best':

- Create a 'best work' baseline. At the beginning of the academic year, ask all learners in your class to complete a piece of work that represents the best they are capable of, both in terms of presentation and attainment. Have this piece of work copied and laminated for reference in their homework book, so that both the child and the parent can see what they are capable of. This should then become the *minimum* standard that is henceforth expected from that particular child. Update the piece at relevant intervals to reflect progress made and to ensure that the baseline remains clear for both parent and child.

- Use the 'before shot/after shot' principle. The idea behind this is to create a clear picture of the progress a learner has made in a specific skill or body of knowledge. The 'before shot' is a baseline assessment that learners complete in order to demonstrate what their capability/ knowledge is before any formal teaching or instruction has taken place. This may take the form of a quiz, series of questions, piece of writing, drawing or diagram – whatever will best demonstrate the pupil's starting point. After instruction and formative feedback, learners complete the same assessment again, the 'after shot', with the second attempt being a clear demonstration of the knowledge, skills and understanding they were able to gain over the course of instruction, as well as any gaps that still exist. This will give parents (or any other stakeholder) clear means to celebrate progress relative to the learner's individual starting point and/or support further work that needs to be done.

FILL PARENTS WITH PRIDE RATHER THAN WORRY

Every day in our classrooms, our learners say, do and produce noteworthy things that never get celebrated beyond the classroom community. Commending these small yet important steps of progress to parents can be a fantastic way to build a more positive home–school relationship, increase the likelihood of active support from home and reduce some of the 'undue worry' for parents that Mick Waters identifies. Try some of the following to help you make positive contact with parents every week (the threshold determined by what you deem to be manageable in relation to the number of learners you teach).

- Sharing a 'comment of the day/week' that has emerged in class discussion.

- Photograph and email home some excellent work in progress that deserves an extra pat on the back.

- Touch base with parents when they have gone over and above in supporting their child on a research or homework task.

- Share an anecdote about how their child has been exceptionally kind or helpful to their peers.

- Let parents know when their child has shown a keen interest in a topic or skill.

These are all pieces of information that would normally go entirely under a parent's radar, but have the capacity to fill them with incredible pride. The means by which you share the positive updates need not be high profile or unduly time consuming: a quick email or phone call, a word at the school gates or a short handwritten note for the student to pass on to their parents is all it takes.

CHAPTER 7

WHAT IS PROGRESS?

WILL ORD

Is it progress if a cannibal is using a knife and fork?

Stanisław Jerzy Lec

WILL ORD is an internationally known trainer and speaker specialising in Philosophy for Children, great learning, mindfulness and school development. He has been a teacher, university lecturer, chair of SAPERE, author, writer for the *TES* and has trained thousands of teachers in twenty-five countries over the last thirteen years. Will provides INSET, keynote speeches and parent–governor evenings.

'Progress' is often seen as education's – perhaps society's – holy grail. It's endlessly demanded of everyone. Understandably so! The idea of learning or developing without progress would be absurd. However, as Lec's delightful quote implies, the concept of progress needs to be carefully and collectively understood by teachers and pupils alike in order for it to be meaningful.

Progress is a concept, and concepts can be investigated in terms of types and levels. We're often obsessed with levels or degrees of progress (Level 4 to 5 or D to C, for example) but equally we can be guilty of ignoring the types of progress. What kinds of progress might there be in the process of learning? Are we looking at advances in knowledge, understanding, processes, motivation, breadth or depth of topic, skills or social/emotional/cognitive abilities? And how do we adapt our evaluations and assessments to cater for each type and in each subject?

The concept of progress is also value laden. Different cultures celebrate certain types of progress and not others. For example, in our education system, progress in some subjects is often valued above others (e.g. maths versus dance). Do we perceive and agree with this value system? What kinds of progress are undervalued or ignored in our schools? How can we avoid the pitfalls of merely valuing what is measureable as opposed to measuring what is really valued?

Many cultures today place great value on 'doing and thinking progress'. Pupils and teachers are continually exhorted to improve their way up the infinite ladder of 'being better'. But how often do adults and children hear the words, 'You know what, you're absolutely fine as you are. Enjoy being yourself! There's no need to change anything at all'? Could developing a healthy sense of 'being enough' or a nourishing peace of mind be seen as a type of progress? Is our progress more towards human doings or human beings?

FURTHER READING

Further information at www.thinkingeducation.co.uk.

PRACTICAL STRATEGIES

CELEBRATING DIFFERENT TYPES OF PROGRESS

■ What types of progress do your learners/colleagues value? Explore the concept of progress with them by getting them to list what they see as the various types of progress in life/learning. Ask them to rank their lists from least to most important and discuss the similarities and differences between their findings.

■ Place five posters around the classroom reading: 'more facts', 'more questions', 'more perspectives', 'more ideas' and 'more confused'. Halfway through a lesson, or at the end, the pupils stand next to the poster that best describes the type of progress they feel they have made during the lesson. Ask them to justify their position by writing examples and explanations on the posters.

■ When might confusion be a symptom of great progress? Make it clear to your learners that feelings of uncertainty or 'stuckness' are a natural part of learning something new and an integral part of moving forward in their understanding. Establish an ethos in your classroom where 'daring to get stuck' or 'stepping into the realm of confusion' is acknowledged to be the beginning of learning, not the end of it!

■ Remember to look out for and celebrate the progress learners make in their motivation levels and their confidence to learn. We often display posters describing levels of attainment, but 'effort scales' which depict and describe levels of effort can be equally helpful. A learner referring to one of these might note that they have moved from 'I can't do it' to 'How do I do it?', or 'I'm not getting work done – I'm distracting others' to 'I'm completing work at a good pace and may be able to reach the extension task before the end of the lesson'. Referring to clear visual descriptors like this enables you to enter into a useful dialogue with learners about their attitudes and helps the learners to reflect meaningfully on their own progress – or, as Will Ord suggests, 'measure what is really valued'.

■ Sometimes one little thing can go wrong for a learner in a classroom and they manage to construct a feeling that the entire lesson has been one big failure for them. The same thing happens to teachers – we can lose all perspective in the face of a difficult experience at work and disregard all the important little successes that punctuated our day. Help learners to stay mindful of what they have achieved by getting them into the habit of reviewing and cataloguing their achievements, either throughout the lesson or at the end. You will probably need to model this process for them. Use this technique to keep them aware that concentrating solely on the things they struggled with can easily cloud their vision of the many things they did accomplish.

CLAIRE GADSBY describes herself as an innovator, educator and motivator. She is a teaching and learning consultant and trainer with more than twenty years of classroom experience and now works with more than 100 schools a year to raise achievement. Much of her work involves working alongside teachers in classrooms where she recommends and demonstrates innovative teaching and learning strategies across the curriculum. Claire is one of the country's leading experts on how to assess without national curriculum levels.

Her specialist expertise also includes practical strategies for demonstrating pupil progress, assessment for learning, active revision, work with gifted and talented pupils, and promoting independent learning. Claire has produced materials for both the Secondary National Strategy and Oxford University Press and has written a book, *Perfect Assessment for Learning* (2012).

CHAPTER 8

A CLIMATE FOR LEARNING

CLAIRE GADSBY

I am genuinely saddened by how hard teachers are working in order to demonstrate pupil progress. Prevalent amongst the profession is the belief, albeit often subconscious, that if we spend a little longer on our lesson planning, or write ever more lengthy comments when marking exercise books, then progress will be evident.

Of course, the truth is that teachers are completely unable to demonstrate pupil progress: that job belongs to the pupil themselves. Ultimately, we need to concern ourselves with creating a classroom culture where metacognitive pupils are the norm; where pupils are able and willing to talk about their own work critically; where conversation, rather than mechanical questioning, prevails; and where pupils are working harder than their teachers. In such classrooms, progress is palpable – you can almost taste it in the air.

Once we are confident that we have created a genuine climate of learning in our classrooms, we might then consider whether we are showcasing pupil progress sufficiently and in all its glory across the fabric and fibre of the school itself. I am excited about the untapped potential of the average classroom and invite you to consider the following:

■ What kind of pupil work gets displayed in your classroom? Is it only the shiny finished article, or do you celebrate process as well as end product, thus helping to create growth mindsets and perseverance?

- ◼ Is the work on display annotated by the pupils themselves, showing where they have been successful and allowing an insight into what Tim Oates (2014) calls the internal, mental life of the child?

- ◼ Do your pupils have access to an 'independence station' where they are actively encouraged to get themselves unstuck without the need for adult intervention? How is success at this level celebrated and collected?

- ◼ Is your classroom rich with photographic evidence of the pupils being successful in all aspects of their learning? Are these photographs annotated to show success at both an academic level and at a deeper holistic level (e.g. interpersonal and cooperative learning skills)?

Great teachers help pupils to make great progress. Let's shout louder about all that success in our classrooms and turn up the volume of our progress song!

FURTHER READING

Gadsby, Claire (2012). *Perfect Assessment for Learning* (Carmarthen: Independent Thinking Press).

Oates, Tim (2014). National Curriculum: Tim Oates On Assessment (video). Available at: https://www.youtube.com/watch?v=-q5vrBXFpm0.

www.clairegadsby.com

PRACTICAL STRATEGIES

PALPABLE PROGRESS

■ In order to embrace the ethos Claire Gadsby describes where 'pupils are working harder than their teachers', it is vital that you are building opportunities to observe the hard work of your learners in action. Be sure to create clear opportunities where you step back from the delivery of information and the role of conduit for all questions to see what your learners can do with the knowledge, skills and information you have given them. Earwig on conversations, look over shoulders and get a sense of what they can do with what you have given them without intervening at each step. During this observation time, you will gain some of the most valuable feedback you can get in your lessons, clearly informing your next steps and also building important independence skills for your learners.

GETTING 'UNSTUCK' INDEPENDENTLY

■ An 'independence station' is a fantastic resource to create a DIY culture when it comes to overcoming 'stuckness' in the classroom. In addition to helpful reference pieces, such as exemplar work, glossaries, sentence stems and research materials, a 'best work book' is a wonderful, ever-changing resource for learners. The best work book is a compilation of some of the most prized pieces of formative and summative work that learners in the class have completed over the course of the academic year, photocopied and laminated for presentation. The merits of the work should be varied and clearly celebrated on each piece. One exemplar may be a breakthrough piece on using key terminology in context, another may be the epitome of excellent presentation of work. The 'best work' that is included need not all be the 'shiny finished article' to which Gadsby refers, but can be work that is exemplary at a variety of stages. Continuously adding pieces as the year progresses is a fantastic way to show the journey of the class through the curriculum, raise the profile of excellent work in the classroom and create a shared reference point for best practice in a variety of forms.

GETTING LEARNERS TO 'TALK ABOUT THEIR OWN WORK CRITICALLY'

■ For certain lessons where you want to be able to talk to each individual about their work, try temporarily organising your classroom so that pupils are seated in an outward-facing horseshoe shape. This is great for when you need learners to be focusing intently on their own independent work while you move around the outside of the horseshoe, having in-depth conversations with each individual about their personal progress. Not only does this arrangement allow the teacher to encourage critical detailed thinking through learner–teacher dialogue, but it can also minimise distractions, as well as allowing learners to have a front row view of those useful displays to which Gadsby refers.

TAPPING THE 'UNTAPPED POTENTIAL'

■ Rather than providing all the input in the initial stages of a new topic, ask learners to work in small groups or pairs to draw out from each other what they already know. To do this you might give them a list of questions they can use such as: what do you definitely know about the topic? How do you know you know it? What do you only *think* you know? Why are you unsure about it? What do you want to know? What further conclusions can we draw by combining the things each of us knows? Learners should record the outcomes of this 'potential-tapping exercise' – perhaps using a visual organiser or chart – and these records can be shared with the class or simply collected in to inform your planning.

CREATING METACOGNITIVE PUPILS

■ To encourage metacognition and help learners to evaluate how familiar they are with a topic they have studied, try showing them three or four fascinating visual stimuli which are ostensibly unconnected to the learning matter. Ask the learners, 'If the topic we've just studied were a picture, which one of these pictures would it be?' By encouraging the learners to make connections between the images and the topic they are studying, you are requiring them to dredge up and consider everything they know about the subject, as well as to view it from different perspectives. You are likely to find that pupils give some surprising responses that will reveal a level of insight into the topic that they didn't even realise they had.

■ Help learners to think carefully about what they have learned, and how they have learned it, by including one false, misleading objective among the lesson's learning objectives. Learners must think hard about what they have learned, analyse their own comprehension and evaluate the process they have undergone in order to identify which of the listed learning objectives they have *not* achieved.

CHAPTER 9

CREATING DESIRABLE DIFFICULTIES TO ENHANCE LEARNING

PROFESSOR ROBERT BJORK

PROFESSOR ROBERT BJORK is a distinguished research professor in the department of psychology at the University of California, Los Angeles. His research focuses on human learning and the implications of the science of learning for optimising instruction. He has served as president of multiple scientific organisations, including the Association for Psychological Science. He is the recipient of various awards, including UCLA's Distinguished Teaching Award, and he is a Fellow of the American Academy of Arts and Sciences.

Instructors and students alike are susceptible to assuming that conditions of instruction which enhance performance during acquisition also enhance long-term learning. This assumption, however, is often questionable and sometimes dramatically wrong: manipulations that make performance improve rapidly during acquisition often fail to support long-term retention and transfer, whereas other manipulations that introduce difficulties, slowing the rate of apparent learning, can enhance post-instruction retention and transfer. Such desirable difficulties (Bjork, 1994) include spacing (rather than massing) repeated study opportunities; interleaving (rather than blocking) practice on separate topics; varying (rather than keeping constant) the manner in which to-be-learned material is presented; and using tests (rather than additional presentations) as learning events.

The distinction between performance (which can be observed) and learning (which must be inferred) is a critical distinction (Soderstrom and Bjork, 2015), and recent research has demonstrated that the potential for learners to be misled by their current performance is very real. Participants tend to prefer conditions that enhance current performance, especially when accompanied by a sense of ease or fluency, even when such conditions produce markedly poorer learning in the long term (Bjork, Dunlosky and Kornell, 2013). Instructors and trainers are also susceptible to choosing conditions of instruction that enhance students' current performance and happiness – such as blocking rather than interleaving, instruction on separate topics or giving non-cumulative final exams.

The desirable difficulties idea, and the body of research on which it rests, provides a foundation for improving teaching and students' learning in potentially dramatic ways (Bjork and Bjork, 2014). Producing the kind of elaborated and inter-linked memory representations that sustain access to knowledge, retard forgetting and enhance transfer, requires that learners be challenged in multiple ways – ways that introduce variability, require generation and tap in to other challenges that prompt learners to be actively involved in the learning process.

FURTHER READING

Bjork, Elizabeth L. and Bjork, Robert A. (2014). Making Things Hard On Yourself, But In a Good Way: Creating Desirable Difficulties to Enhance Learning. In Morton A. Gernsbacher and James R. Pomerantz (eds), *Psychology and the Real World: Essays Illustrating Fundamental Contributions to Society* (2nd edn) (New York: Worth), pp. 59–68.

Bjork, Robert A. (1994). Memory and Metamemory Considerations in the Training of Human Beings. In Janet Metcalfe and Arthur P. Shimamura (eds), *Metacognition: Knowing About Knowing* (Cambridge, MA: MIT Press), pp. 185–205.

Bjork, Robert A., Dunlosky, John and Kornell, Nate (2013). Self-Regulated Learning: Beliefs, Techniques, and Illusions. *Annual Review of Psychology* 64: 417–444.

Soderstrom, Nicholas C. and Bjork, Robert A. (2015). Learning versus Performance: An Integrative Review. *Perspectives on Psychological Science* 10: 176–199.

PRACTICAL STRATEGIES

INTERLEAVING

■ We might naturally assume that concentrating on discrete topics (or aspects of topics) for a sustained period of time before moving on to the next topic is the most effective way to teach. However, Robert Bjork's research suggests that mixing up or 'interleaving' topics or skills can help people to retain their learning much better in the long term. For example, rather than studying poems, artists, muscle groups, dance moves and so on one at a time and in great depth, a teacher might try to structure their teaching to dip in and out of these over a number of lessons, revisiting and reconsidering each topic or skill each time as part of an assortment. If practicalities allow, you might also like to try varying the location when you revisit a topic. This has been shown to help learners become accustomed to accessing the relevant information more easily, even when they are away from their usual classroom and in different situations.

SPACING

■ When teaching factual knowledge, long-term recall can be improved by allowing learners to study something a number of times over a longer time span, rather than repeatedly studying it over a shorter time span (cramming). Practising the actual act of retrieving the information helps us to retrieve it more easily next time, so while we might think that those frequent little tests are just for our benefit as teachers – to assess understanding and inform planning – they are, in fact, extremely useful for our learners too. Students will have to force themselves to recall their learning if you ask them to summarise it for homework or immediately after a classroom activity, rather than allowing them to take notes or copy down while receiving the information.

CHALLENGING LEARNERS IN MULTIPLE WAYS

■ Be careful not to pigeonhole a pupil as only being able to learn in a certain way. No matter how they might prefer to be taught, learners are more likely to hold on to information if they experience it and process it in different ways. Likewise, teachers should avoid relying on a default way of teaching a familiar topic time after time. Vary the methods you use to present the same piece of information to your learners and allow them to condense and consolidate that learning in different forms. Rather than asking learners to revisit information simply by rereading material (passively absorbing it) or taking their usual notes, you might revisit to-be-learned information in the form of a puzzle so that they have to work harder to recall it (e.g. unscrambling key vocabulary or filling in blanks).

CHAPTER 10

PROGRESS AND PRACTICE

PROFESSOR JOHN WEST-BURNHAM

PROFESSOR JOHN WEST-BURNHAM is a writer, teacher and consultant in education leadership with a particular interest in leadership learning and development and innovative approaches to learning in schools and communities. He has been a schoolteacher, teacher trainer, education officer and has held posts in six universities. John is the author or editor of twenty-eight books, including *Understanding Leadership* (with Libby Nicholas, 2016) and *Leadership Dialogues* (with Dave Harris, 2015), and he has worked in twenty-seven countries. He is Honorary Professor of Education at the University of Worcester.

Progress in any field of human activity is the result of the appropriate combination of a number of complex variables – intrinsic motivation, ability, appropriate teaching and coaching and practice. Practice is sometimes demonised as being rote learning by another name, but in reality it is very difficult to conceptualise meaningful and sustainable progress without a commitment to practice.

In essence, practice gives the learner the confidence that comes from the mastery of information, the building blocks of knowledge, a repertoire of skills and techniques, and the need to embed understanding so that it becomes intuitive. Any professional musician, athlete, dancer or craftsperson will stress the importance of regular routines and, crucially, effort and application – what Carol Dweck (2008) has described as a 'growth mindset'.

The concert violinist Nicola Benedetti describes her work as creating the 'feeling of enrichment that comes from making an effort'. She explains: 'If I stick with one annoying finger movement, I know that the feeling the child will get at the end, when it works, is better than just being quickly satisfied by novelty.' Benedetti says that children from different backgrounds are always amazed by the fact she has to practise for four to six hours a day: 'There are no shortcuts' (see Thorpe, 2013).

Simplistically, practice involves repetition in order to develop memory – whether kicking a ball or remembering the periodic table. Practice is equally true of language development: the more we use vocabulary, the greater the confidence we develop in using it; the more we practise speaking, the more fluent we become – and it's essentially the same if we are 5 or 50.

However, practice of itself is not enough to ensure progress, hence the importance of feedback. Feedback, using the Dweck model of growth mindsets, ensures that practice is developmental and secures and consolidates incremental improvement. Perhaps we need to allow more time for learners to practise, to enhance confidence and a sense of control, and so develop a heightened sense of personal efficacy.

FURTHER READING

Dweck, Carol (2008). *Mindset: The New Psychology of Success* (New York: Ballantine Books).

Nicholas, Libby and West-Burnham, John (2016). *Understanding Leadership: Challenges and Reflections* (Carmarthen: Crown House Publishing).

Thorpe, Vanessa (2013). Stick to One Instrument, Violinist Nicola Benedetti Tells Pushy Parents, *The Guardian* (5 May). Available at: http://www.theguardian.com/education/2013/may/05/nicola-benedetti-violin-pushy-parents.

West-Burnham, John and Harris, Dave (2015). *Leadership Dialogues: Conversations and Activities for Leadership Teams* (Carmarthen: Crown House Publishing).

www.johnwest-burnham.co.uk

PRACTICAL STRATEGIES

MASTERING INFORMATION: THE KEY TO GAINING CONFIDENCE

■ One way to help learners master a concept is to get them to review and condense their learning. Give your class black marker pens and ask them to 'black out' words in the text they have read, so that the flow of the piece still retains its original meaning but the superfluous words are removed. Once they have done this, ask them to repeat the process, this time removing further words to reduce the text down to its core messages. Each time learners have read through their newly censored version, encourage them to condense it even further into fewer and fewer words. Finally, ask them to consider which five words they will leave visible to convey the text's full meaning as succinctly as possible.

PRACTICE AND REPETITION

■ Embedding knowledge, skills and information, and the practice required to achieve this, can be met with ceiling-scraping eye-rolls and exasperated sighs when it is done in the same way over and over again. One of the factors West-Burnham asserts that best facilitates progress is 'appropriate teaching', and part of this is the acknowledgement that the best way for learners to practise is by creating different learning opportunities to encounter the same information. Try using the 'pyramid principle' to achieve this. Here, learners undertake the first stage as an individual, recording their initial thoughts, ideas and knowledge. They then move on to a paired structure, where they share/develop/combine/embed ideas through discussion with one peer. Pairs can then move into small groups, where they need to consolidate the ideas of the pairings into a larger visual representation which can be shared with the class. Allow learners to choose a medium that best suits the length/breadth of their ideas and the thinking process of their group to record these findings.

■ Occasionally plan a lesson where there is a designated interval (perhaps just five minutes) for 'deliberate practice'. This is where learners spend a short, controlled amount of time working repeatedly on a very specific skill or concept that they personally need to develop. Whether it be writing out a spelling, repeating a particular move in sport, pronouncing a tricky phrase in MFL or reciting key dates in history, the act of deliberate practice moves the learners towards a state where they can perform these tasks automatically, without even having to think hard about them. This kind of practice can feel tiresome in its repetitiveness, but by ring fencing a short spell in the lesson that everyone understands is dedicated solely to this activity, learners can experience a sense of urgency when attempting to beat their own personal best several times over, knowing that the time in which to do so is strictly limited.

INTRINSIC MOTIVATION AND MINDSET

- Once learners have a clear understanding of their learning destination or personal goal, ask them to produce their own 'success flowchart' in picture or word form. This diagram can be used to help each learner anticipate what difficulties they might encounter on the learning journey and plot out in advance the techniques they plan to use to overcome those difficulties. Learners can then refer to their flowchart throughout the learning experience, documenting their milestones in order to review and celebrate their own progress. They require each learner to prepare effectively for the process they are engaged in, as well as remaining cognisant of their own methods, effort and advancements.

PROFESSOR GUY CLAXTON is visiting professor of education at King's College London. He is the originator of Building Learning Power and the author of many books on teaching and learning including *What's the Point of School?* (2008), *The Learning Powered School* (with Maryl Chambers, Graham Powell and Bill Lucas, 2011) and *Educating Ruby: What Our Children Really Need to Learn* (with Bill Lucas, 2015).

CHAPTER 11

BUILDING LEARNING POWER: FINDING YOUR OWN SWEET SPOT

PROFESSOR GUY CLAXTON

Fifteen 12-year-olds from the Sunderland Football Academy are engaged in a routine training activity. But as they persist, they start to check with each other as to whether what they are doing is too easy, too hard or just right. When they agree it has become too easy, they quickly change the rules to make it a bit harder. Their coach, Elliot Dickman, has trained the boys to be aware of their learning 'sweet spot' – when they are being challenged but not overstretched – and to think like coaches, so they can adjust the level of difficulty of their training for themselves. Too easy and it's boring; too hard and it's demoralising. Learning happens best in the sweet spot – and nobody knows where that shifting spot is better than the learners themselves.

The same happens when you go to the gym. Each machine can be customised so that everyone is getting the right level of stretch for them. As they get stronger, they can up the level of difficulty; provided they are sensitive to their own bodies, nobody needs to hover over them telling them when and how to 'differentiate'. And it's the same with learning and the mind. Students can be helped to become their own 'mind coaches', monitoring the mental stretch that an activity is giving them and adjusting it accordingly. In the conventional approach to differentiation, teachers have to guess where the sweet spot is; in the Building Learning Power (BLP) approach to teaching, we help children learn how to do that monitoring and adjusting for themselves. It takes time for them to build up their 'learning muscles' so they can gradually take on more responsibility for themselves.

It takes a confident teacher to progressively share more and more of the responsibility for designing activities with their learners. But it's worth it. As students become more powerful learners, capable of handling greater responsibility, so teaching becomes more satisfying – and more fun. Who wouldn't rather be surrounded by turbo-charged young learners – unafraid of challenge and raring to go – rather than children who are passive, dependent or anxious?

FURTHER READING

Claxton, Guy (2002). *Building Learning Power: Helping Young People Become Better Learners* (Bristol: TLO Ltd).

Claxton, Guy, Chambers, Maryl, Powell, Graham and Lucas, Bill (2011). *The Learning Powered School: Pioneering 21st Century Education* (Bristol: TLO Ltd).

Claxton, Guy and Lucas, Bill (2015). *Educating Ruby: What Our Children Really Need to Learn* (Carmarthen: Crown House Publishing).

Resources at www.buildinglearningpower.co.uk.

PRACTICAL STRATEGIES

ADJUSTING AND MONITORING INDEPENDENTLY

■ Install a 'riskometer' in the classroom (like the one on page 101). Ask learners to identify how 'too hard', 'too easy' and 'just right' feel, and write up their descriptions. When prompted to assess how challenged they have felt, younger learners are often quick to tell their teachers that they found the work 'easy' (because they feel that this assessment has the most impressive status)! Making your riskometer a high profile reference tool in the classroom will help learners to understand that attempting to stretch and challenge oneself carries more classroom kudos than finding things easy.

■ Design activities that allow learners to adjust the difficulty. For example, instead of dishing out a page

THE RISKOMETER

'This was a few steps too hard. Next time I will choose a more manageable task.'

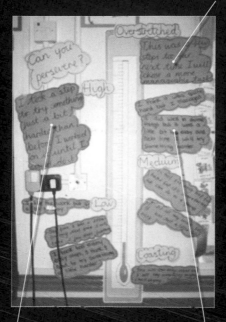

'I took a step to try something just a bit harder than before. I worked on it until I could do it.'

'I did well in most things but it was a little bit too easy and next time I will try something harder.'

of multiplication problems, have learners work in pairs to create their own problems, discovering how difficult they can make them while still supplying the correct answer.

■ When pupils have home learning to do, allow them to choose (within limits) how adventurous they want to be. Agree with them a numerical scale that indicates the subjective level of difficulty they chose (e.g. 1.1 to 1.9). When you mark their work, multiply your 'success' mark by their 'risk' mark to get the final score – just like they do in diving competitions (you'll soon have a class of learning Tom Daleys on your hands!).

THE SHIFTING SWEET SPOT

■ Apply a 'low threshold, high ceiling' principle to open-ended tasks. This means ensuring that the task set provides scope for all learners to access and engage with it, yet also provides latitude for all learners to challenge themselves by making more insightful connections and reaching for ever more sophisticated levels of response. In this way, learners are, of course, naturally encouraged to find what Professor Claxton calls the 'sweet spot'. An open-ended odd-one-out activity (without a binary right/ wrong answer) can be an excellent way to achieve this:

some selections may be more obvious or qualitative (low threshold), while others may include lateral connections or interpretation (high ceiling). Either way, learners are forced to catalogue what they understand about the selection of objects/images/words/numbers presented to them in order to make a justified assertion about which one the odd one out might be.

JAMES NOTTINGHAM worked as a teacher and leader in primary and secondary schools in the UK before co-founding an award-winning, multimillion pound regeneration project supporting education and public and voluntary organisations across north-east England.

He is the founder and executive director of Challenging Learning which has offices in Europe and Australia. He is well known throughout Scandinavia for his work with John Hattie's Visible Learning, and internationally he is recognised for his work on challenge, progress, Philosophy for Children and the Learning Pit.

His first book, *Challenging Learning* (2010), has been published in five languages and has received widespread critical acclaim. His follow-up book, *Encouraging Learning* (2013), supports his work with parents and community groups as well as with teachers and leaders. He is currently writing a series of books to share the best strategies for feedback, challenge, dialogue, progress and metacognition.

CHAPTER 12

PROGRESS, PROGRESS, PROGRESS

JAMES NOTTINGHAM

Let's say a student gets ten out of ten in the test. Would you praise that student? Would you say 'well done'? I'm guessing most of us would probably say yes. However, what if that test had been so easy that the student in question could have got everything right with his eyes closed? Should we still say 'well done' then? Maybe the answer is still yes, but just think of the problems that might create: it might lead the student to believe that what we care about most is that he gets everything right. He might believe that we don't care whether he's learned anything or not – just so long as he gets ten out of ten. This particular slippery slope often leads students to seek easy options; to take the path of least resistance; to avoid challenging tasks in the belief that easy praise is better than difficult learning. Or, as Norman Vincent Peale once said: 'The trouble with most of us is that we'd rather be ruined by praise than saved by criticism.'

Instead of praising these 'achievement scores', I would suggest that the better option is to praise 'progress scores'. Do a pre-test first. Call this a survey if your students don't like the word test! Whatever you call it, the idea is to find out how many answers your students know already and therefore how much room for improvement they each have.

So, for example, if there are some students who currently know less than 50% of the answers, then you know they have plenty of room to improve. For the students who already know most of the answers and don't have much room to make progress, you now know to set them additional challenges.

Now, when you come to give the 'actual' test (the summative assessment), you will be able to calculate their progress score (the difference between the pre-test and the actual test). And it is the progress score that is worth praising. Not the pre-test score, not the actual test score, but the *progress* score.

Of course, progress isn't just something that can be shown through tests. For example, it can be drawn attention to by displaying photographs of earlier drafts alongside completed artwork. Or by colour-coding so that first drafts are done in one colour, edits in a second colour and then final pieces in a third colour. Or it can be shown in videos of earlier attempts so that students can reflect together on the progress they've made from the start to now.

The point is: shouldn't our pupils be coming to school to improve what they can do, and not just to prove?

FURTHER READING

Nottingham, James (2013). *Encouraging Learning: How You Can Help Children Learn* (Oxford: Routledge).

Nottingham, James (2015). *Challenging Learning: Theory, Effective Practice and Lesson Ideas to Create Optimal Learning in the Classroom* (Oxford: Routledge).

www.challenginglearning.com

@JamesNottingham

PRACTICAL STRATEGIES

PRAISING PROGRESS

James Nottingham's idea of praising progress, rather than scores, can be an excellent way to motivate learners not simply to pass a test, but instead to make the best progress they possibly can. Using this kind of tailored feedback will ensure that the formative work that ensues will challenge learners relative to their starting points, as opposed to according to the level we assume they are starting from.

Try some of these alternative ways of raising the profile of progress:

■ When providing feedback on formative assessments, place the emphasis on the number of marks by which the learner has missed the next grade boundary/level/stage/their own target level rather than simply reporting their raw score. This shifts the focus to where they should be aiming for next time, rather than simply accepting their current level of achievement.

■ After they have received clear feedback on an assessed piece of work, ask the class (or small groups) to prepare an 'examiner's report' that creates a master list of the kinds of gaps that have emerged in the collective performance of the class. Students will then be able to see how their own personal gaps (and successes) compare to their peers. A potential follow-on could be for students to seek out peers with similar gaps to their own to put together an action plan or complete a tailored challenge for closing those gaps. The focus of the reflective exercise is to raise the profile of the successes that have been achieved and also to look with a progress-oriented eye at what needs to happen next.

■ Another reflective exercise that can help students to consider their own progress closely is self-reported grades. Before beginning an assessment piece, ask learners to predict what mark/grade/outcome they expect to achieve. Moving beyond a simple level prediction into identifying which elements of the assessed piece they anticipate they will excel at and which elements they expect to find more difficult can provide an even more focused forecast of their achievement.

AVOIDING 'THE SLIPPERY SLOPE' AND 'THE PATH OF LEAST RESISTANCE'

■ Try allocating five minutes of each lesson to building up a better picture of one particular learner. Over the course of several lessons you will be able to construct a 'learning portrait' of each pupil in your class. Take this special time to talk to that individual and study their work. What do they find too easy? Do they embrace challenges or avoid them? What types of challenge do they shy away from? What specific improvements are there between their first piece of work and their last? Where do you need to set the goalposts in order to make sure they have enough room for improvement? This will allow you to 'reflect together on the progress they've made'. Having this practice as a routine in your lessons helps learners to realise that they can't slip under your radar and 'seek the easiest options' in the long term. It also reminds us to focus on individual progress rather than whole-class progress towards standardised tests.

CHAPTER 13

LEARNING WITHOUT LIMITS

MARK BURNS

MARK BURNS taught full-time for twelve years. His subsequent work over the last eight years has seen him co-develop and work intensively on the Osiris 'Outstanding Teaching Intervention' with literally thousands of primary and secondary teachers to improve the quality of teaching and learning in their classrooms. The impact of this programme has been noted by dozens of Ofsted reports as contributing to the improved performance of schools. He has also co-written two best-selling books. The first, *Engaging Learners* (2012) has sold more than 30,000 copies worldwide and has been translated into several other languages. The follow-up *Teaching Backwards* was released in November 2014. His work with schools has been twice shortlisted for the *TES* Awards.

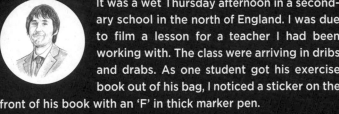

It was a wet Thursday afternoon in a secondary school in the north of England. I was due to film a lesson for a teacher I had been working with. The class were arriving in dribs and drabs. As one student got his exercise book out of his bag, I noticed a sticker on the front of his book with an 'F' in thick marker pen.

'What's that?' I asked him.

'It's my aspirational target grade, Sir,' was his dejected response. 'Who knows, my teacher says if I work hard I might even get an E.'

This student's apathy was understandable, and yet in the same school only the next day I was privileged to sit in on a lesson where a quite different approach was yielding radically different outcomes. The teacher told me that she refused to accept the target grades that her learners had been given. Her argument was that it would be a self-fulfilling prophecy. If she gave them C grade work to complete in class, they would end up with C grades. Instead, her approach was to teach them all A* material and provide the support and scaffolding for those who needed assistance. She said, 'If some of them end up with a B grade, instead of reaching A*, then they will still have done well. After all, no one in this room is supposedly targeted higher than a C.'

This teacher is one of the hundreds of 'outliers' who have fascinated me throughout the course of my work over the last eight years, working intensively with teachers nationwide. These outliers are teachers whose results are consistently and hugely better than their peers, year in, year out, despite teaching the same children as their colleagues who possibly yield less aspirational results. They do so by refusing to allow the prior attainment of learners to cap their future learning potential. Instead, these teachers consider how to overcome the obstacles that will potentially stop learners from moving from their current level of attainment to the beautiful outcomes they hope for their class to achieve. They then plan and teach so that learners are able to achieve them.

Michelangelo could have been neatly summing up their approach to differentiation when he (supposedly) wrote: 'The greatest danger for most of us is not that our aim is too high and we miss it, but that it is too low and we reach it.'

FURTHER READING

Griffith, Andy and Burns, Mark (2012). *Engaging Learners: Outstanding Teaching* (Carmarthen: Crown House Publishing).

Griffith, Andy and Burns, Mark (2014). *Teaching Backwards: Outstanding Teaching* (Carmarthen: Crown House Publishing).

PRACTICAL STRATEGIES

Mark Burns' anecdote highlights an interesting point about the potential impact of cognitive bias on classroom practice.

REJECT SELF-FULFILLING PROPHECIES

- Avoid labelling learners (consciously or otherwise) as 'less able'. Descriptions like these – even if used only in the staffroom – can inadvertently affect the opportunities that we afford pupils, the level of challenge that we give them access to and even the effort that we expect of them. Instead, use a less constraining term such as 'low attaining'. Since the acquiring of skill, knowledge and understanding is a progressive journey, a low-attainer might eventually become a high-attainer through enhanced opportunity or effort.

- Don't cap low-attainers by denying them access to more difficult work. When designing a task for a group of learners who are at very different starting points, ensure that the task has integral 'layers' of increasing difficulty. This way, all learners are encouraged to push upwards, continually reaching for those layers that present the most appropriate challenge for their individual needs. For a team task, you might even allocate an appropriate number of points for each layer of challenge (e.g. one point for each item correctly placed on the diagram, two points for each item accurately labelled, three points for each annotation that explains the function of an item). By allocating points to the different levels of difficulty, you are encouraging your highest attainers to immediately reach for the higher scoring challenges, while less confident learners still have every right to attempt a harder task and potentially win more points for their team if they so wish. No one is limited by lack of opportunity.

OVERCOMING GAPS IN KNOWLEDGE, UNDERSTANDING AND SKILLS

Working in an inner city primary school some time ago, the children were asked by their teacher to write about what it would be like to stand on a beach on a stormy day. For those children lucky enough to have been taken to the coast on holidays or day trips, they had the necessary life experiences to complete this task to a high standard. For those less fortunate, it was nigh on impossible. As one child said to me when I asked him why he was struggling to write much, 'I've never been to the seaside.'

Ask yourself, what are the specific knowledge, skills or understanding gaps that could stop all learners from reaching that beautiful outcome? What resources, support materials, background knowledge and targeted teaching could I provide that would enable those learners to bridge these gaps?

SIGNPOST THE PITFALLS

If you have the benefit of having taught a particular module of learning before, consider the pitfalls or specific areas of difficulty where certain learners are likely to get stuck. How can you model and explain these areas more clearly so that learners negotiate them successfully?

MARTIN ROBINSON worked for twenty years in state schools in London as a teacher, a leader and an advanced skills teacher. Now an education consultant, he works with schools on enhancing their pupils' knowledge acquisition, questioning and communication skills. He also speaks regularly on creativity, character and a wide range of other current concerns in education.

CHAPTER 14

THE PUPIL'S PROGRESS

MARTIN ROBINSON

Whoso beset him round
With dismal stories,
Do but themselves confound.

John Bunyan, *The Pilgrim's Progress*

For the pupil, progress relies on hope, a belief in a journey towards a point of completion and an idea that ultimate salvation is just one more bit of effort away. This promised land, in which there shall be 'seraphims and cherubims' and an eternal life of joy, will be won when the child has moved from a state of incompletion towards the superior state of 'got some good exam grades'. Physically, a child starts school small and finishes it tall – progress has clearly been made. Academically, you start school without any certificates and you end with an EBacc and an A level or two – or, God forbid, a vocational qualification – as you trudge towards the closed factory gate or the newly opened call centre. Rather than a heavenly pursuit, a pupil's progress is tied to these rather mundane goals.

Teachers have algorithms to set their pupils targets. They distribute these goals like manna from heaven and report 'If Jacinta wishes to progress to a B grade she will need to knuckle down and work hard until the exam.' Then they track her progress towards that goal. This has become the extent of their ambition, justified by the belief that the B grade in such and such a subject will get her a job in animal husbandry or law or a part-time job in a beauty salon. The belief in progress is underpinned by a dour utopian utility.

Most children make expected progress, which therefore isn't really progress at all – it is doing as expected. So why is it fetishised so much? Because it can be measured, and if the underprivileged make more progress than the privileged then all the value added boxes will be ticked, and all will have really achieved (except the privileged who will have underperformed), and the bastions of privilege will come crashing to the ground, and all will surrender to the new meritocratic reality: the meek will inherit the earth.

But this won't happen.

And nor should it.

Progress is anathema to a humane education. It is bowing out of our responsibility towards each other by sacrificing education on the altar of hope in a suburban heaven on earth, which is always one more qualification away from where we think perfection is attainable – but only by adding an extra GCSE, BA, PGCE, MA or a Ph effing D ... Education = inflation, inflation, inflation.

Instead of the hubris of ever marching progress we need to learn how to remain still, how to be us in the here and now. Teachers can't make the future for their pupils; they must allow them to make it for themselves. Teachers should introduce pupils to the best that has been thought, said and done, and enable their charges to begin to add to the best that has been thought, said and done; initiate them into how to use judgement, discernment and discrimination; introduce them to past successes and mistakes; and share with them that humanity is a flawed state of being. No matter how perfect we believe our systems to be, teachers should not spend all their energies supporting systems of progress that insist pupils sacrifice themselves to the demands of a mechanistic target grade, with its accompanying objectives and computer-generated statements. The subject matter that is taught is more important and interesting than any grade; discovery and adventure are more important than the progress myth and its simplistic goals.

Pupils need to practise in order to live a good life, so support them in forever becoming. Teach, don't track. Focus on ideas, knowledge, practice and debate, and not grades. Encourage children to do something now, for its own sake, and not in the mistaken belief that it will make them a better person, get them a better job or help them progress towards a far off, dull and distinctly obtainable goal. Instead of these dismal stories, offer them adventure in the never-ending pursuit of wisdom.

FURTHER READING

Robinson, Martin (2013). *Trivium 21c: Preparing Young People for the Future with Lessons from the Past* (Carmarthen: Independent Thinking Press).

Robinson, Martin (2016). *Trivium in Practice* (Carmarthen: Independent Thinking Press).

PRACTICAL STRATEGIES

UNTYING OURSELVES FROM 'MUNDANE GOALS'

How do you ensure that young, impressionable minds don't see learning in your classroom simply as a string of tasks to be completed because the teacher or the curriculum says so? Martin Robinson highlights here how a target- and assessment-driven culture in schools can lead pupils (and teachers) to feel that learning is a mundane journey they must doggedly take, when, in fact, the acquiring of new knowledge should be experienced as a great adventure – one which might branch off in endless possibilities.

You can avoid this problem by taking a careful look at your schemes of work:

- Are there places where depth of subject matter is being sacrificed for the mechanistic ticking off of targets? Does the programme of study allow full appreciation of the topic or does it present an abridged/censored version? Try introducing learners to 'the best that has been thought, said and done' by presenting a key artist, writer, thinker, scientist, etc. and asking learners to research, present on and debate the question: 'Who was this person and why are they important to what we are studying?'

- Do the tasks focus on helping pupils to genuinely accumulate and develop ideas, skills and knowledge, or could any of them be seen as simply 'filler' exercises? Asking learners to 'design a poster on Judaism', for example, may not develop any further their understanding of Judaism or indeed their poster-designing skills. A well-planned assessment piece should be one where learners are making conscious choices about the skills and information they use and the way in which they communicate it. Rather than producing work simply for an assessment grade, create opportunities wherever possible for pupils to offer their classwork up for comment from their classmates so that they can debate, defend or revise the choices they have made in their work.

DISCOVERY AND ADVENTURE

■ To help every learner in a large class to question, debate and ponder the subject in hand, try using a 'silent discussion'. For this, you should provide large sheets of paper for students to debate a topic using only the medium of writing to communicate. Allow students to move silently around the written debates, reading other groups' comments and adding their own ideas, reactions and responses. In this scenario, every member of the class is given equal opportunity to 'voice' their opinion in the debate and everyone is exposed to a multitude of diverse opinions. Some pupils may initially focus more on absorbing other classmates' ideas and simply validate others' points with simple affirmations like 'I agree' – but this mode of participation has its own part to play and should not be devalued by default.

■ An effective way to give learners a sense of possibility, discovery and adventure is to leave your lesson on a deliberately tantalising cliffhanger. Encourage learners' creativity and ignite their curiosity by withholding the answer to a particularly intriguing question 'until next time'. Alternatively, you might provide a clue as to what might happen in the next part of this learning escapade and encourage pupils to ponder and anticipate.

ENCOURAGING 'THE NEVER-ENDING PURSUIT OF WISDOM'

■ Your own delight in the adventure of learning and the enthusiasm transmitted by that is a powerful tool when teaching others. Find ways to celebrate the discoveries that you and your pupils make. Try updating your pupils regularly on what your latest bedtime reading book is – giving them a little information about it to spark curiosity. Establish a pinboard in your classroom or an online forum where pupils can share their further reading, encounters, thoughts and questions about a topic of interest with each other.

CHAPTER 15

EXEMPLAR WORK

MIKE GERSHON

What does progress look like?

As teachers, we tend to have a good idea.

But what about our students?

If they are not certain, then progress will be harder to achieve. Ambiguity diffuses effort. It can also generate a sense of uncertainty. This makes it harder to stay motivated. Not knowing what the goal looks like makes the path more difficult to follow.

This leads us to the central premise that opening up success criteria makes progress a more likely prospect for all students.

One of the most effective ways through which to do this is the provision of exemplar work. This is work which demonstrates what it means to meet one or more of the success criteria for a given task or activity.

It can also be work which demonstrates how not to fulfil the success criteria! In this case, the work becomes a negative model – something to work hard to avoid instead of imitate.

You can get exemplar work from a number of sources. One option is to keep work produced by your current cohort and use this the following year. Another option is to create it yourself or, if appropriate, use the examples which some exam boards provide.

A final option is to use work produced by students in your current class. For example, you might photocopy a piece which exemplifies how to make significant progress in a short space of time, annotate this and then share it with your class through a discussion exercise.

However you choose to use exemplar work, the effect will be the same. Students will have a clearer sense of what progress looks like, the success criteria will have been opened up for them and they will have a model to which they can refer when producing their own work.

FURTHER READING

Gershon, Mike. 'How to ... Great Classroom Teaching' series. See http://mikegershon.com/books-and-publications/.

Gershon, Mike. 'Quick 50' series. See http://mikegershon.com/quick-50-series/.

Hymer, Barry and Gershon, Mike (2014). *Growth Mindset Pocketbook* (Alresford: Teachers' Pocketbooks).

www.mikegershon.com

PRACTICAL STRATEGIES

As Mike Gershon points out, if we don't make explicitly clear to our learners the ingredients that go into forging a successful outcome, then some learners may 'meet one or more of the success criteria' simply by chance, while others will fail entirely to make the progress they could have achieved if they'd had clearer direction.

REMOVING AMBIGUITY

■ Provide a checklist that learners can use as a reference point before, during and after they undertake a piece of work. Prior to submitting their completed work, learners must evaluate it against the list of criteria and ensure they can confidently tick each box. It can be useful for learners to use colour-coded highlighting, in-margin annotations or – for art work – sticky notes to show where they feel they have met the particular goals you have specified. This keeps learners focused on the success criteria.

■ Ask colleagues who teach the same assignments as you to provide you with a list of 'bad practice' they have noted in their pupils' work. Use this information, together with your own notes, to compile a report – one to be shared with learners across classes – of pitfalls to avoid in this type of work. You might even use the report to generate your own 'negative model' that demonstrates, in an amusing way, what *not* to do.

WHAT DOES PROGRESS LOOK LIKE?

■ Use a digital camera to capture examples of great work and create an online gallery of these pieces that learners can peruse to assist them with their homework. Showing multiple examples of high-scoring work will reduce the risk of learners simply copying one great example they are shown or producing too-close a replica.

■ Use a visualiser during your lesson to display a piece of excellent work on the class board for learners to scrutinise, discuss and develop.

OPEN UP SUCCESS CRITERIA

■ Give learners several examples of exemplar work and ask them to complete a 'spot the similarities' exercise, where they must scrutinise the excellent pieces and pick out things they all have in common. In doing this, they will be automatically generating a list of success criteria which they can then use to inform their own work.

■ Present learners with a selection of work samples at varying levels of quality. Using the concept of the well-known Top Trumps card game, ask learners to score the pieces of work against each of the success criteria. In true Top Trumps style, a mark out of ten can be given for each 'category', so that pupils are evaluating the various strengths and weaknesses of each piece in an informed and useful way.

■ Get pupils to place transparencies over a written 'negative model' and, using a transparency marking pen, make suggestions, corrections and additions. Each learner can then compare their own annotated overlay with that of a classmate.

■ Does the success of the piece of work rely on the learners following a series of steps? If so, you can ask every pupil to produce their own mini best practice model by releasing each stage of the task in carefully managed steps over a set period of time, as opposed to sharing the entire task from the outset – for example, sentence by sentence to compile a perfect opening paragraph for a given style of report, step by step for a mathematical process or even a methodical approach to deciphering a poem or analysing a source. Each time a learner successfully completes a small step, you release the next step to them. At the end of this exercise, every learner should have a model (and a mental blueprint) for the exact process they will need to follow whenever they have to complete a similar sort of task independently.

PAM HOOK is an educational consultant who developed a unique classroom-based approach using SOLO taxonomy to make learning visible. She has published many books and articles on using this approach in teaching and learning. Pam works with schools to develop curricula and pedagogies for learning to learn. She writes curriculum material for government and business, has directed New Zealand Ministry of Education contracts and is co-author of two science textbooks widely used in New Zealand secondary schools. She is a popular keynote speaker at conferences.

CHAPTER 16

ON MAKING PROGRESS VISIBLE WITH SOLO

PAM HOOK

After making a query in Google, I am offered 'previous' and 'next' page views. I can see where my search started, where I have been and where I can go next. My progress in searching is visible and my next steps (albeit chosen by the PageRank algorithm) are accessible.

Teachers and students must rely on their own set of assumptions or working models to make progress in learning visible. These assumptions and working models influence, for better or worse, the way students learn and teachers teach. For example, if we work from the assumption that learning is serendipitous or that intelligence is fixed, we can limit our expectations for progress.

I believe that SOLO taxonomy (Biggs and Collis, 1982) is a powerful model for making progress in learning visible for teachers and students. In doing so, it also raises their expectations for progress.

SOLO gives teachers and students a common language for progress – encompassing no idea, an idea, ideas, related ideas and extended ideas. Quantitative progress is shown by SOLO prestructural, unistructural and multistructural levels; qualitative progress is shown by SOLO relational and extended abstract levels.

Task and outcome can be at different levels of SOLO. This independence allows teachers and students to identify how students progress in both the complexity of the learning intentions they attempt and the complexity of the learning outcomes they achieve.

Finally, there is no race to the top with SOLO. Instead, progress is represented by a metaphoric spiral: over time, learners accumulate deeper understanding as they continually revisit the SOLO levels, reinterpreting new ideas and integrating them with what they already know. SOLO is a model that assumes progress is ongoing; it assumes we will never stop learning.

FURTHER READING

Biggs, John B. and Collis, Kevin F. (1982). *Evaluating the Quality of Learning: The SOLO Taxonomy* (New York: Academic Press).

Hook, Pam (2016). *First Steps with SOLO Taxonomy: Applying the Model in Your Classroom* (Laughton: Essential Resources).

Hook, Pam and Mills, Julie. *SOLO Taxonomy: A Guide for Schools Bk1* (Laughton: Essential Resources).

Hook, Pam and Mills, Julie. *SOLO Taxonomy: A Guide for Schools Bk2* (Laughton: Essential Resources).

http://pamhook.com

PRACTICAL STRATEGIES

Using consistent, clear discourse about how you measure and discuss progress in your classroom is an important part of learners understanding how and where they are making advancements in their learning. Without this, as Pam Hook emphasises, there are opportunities for complacency and limited progression.

QUANTITATIVE LEARNING VS. QUALITATIVE LEARNING

■ Building up the initial 'blocks' of learning (which Hook describes as the 'quantitative' level) is an important part of the learning process to firmly embed before attempting more challenging connections. The use of recall cards is a great way to allow learners to become proficient with the information that they encounter at the unistructural and multistructural levels of SOLO taxonomy, working independently and at their own pace. Cards are prepared (either by the teacher or by the learners themselves) with direct questions about the topic on one side of the card and the answer on the reverse.

All cards are placed question side up on the table and learners quiz themselves on the key terms/concepts/

ideas. If they are at the prestructural level, having no knowledge about the answers to the questions in front of them, they will be able to move quickly to the unistructural and multistructural levels as they turn the cards over and reveal the answers. Learners continue to quiz themselves, turning the cards over first one way and then back again until they are no longer making errors in their answers to the questions in front of them.

Once learners are secure in their multistructural understanding, the same cards can be used to begin making relational connections. Learners can start by choosing two cards to turn over and challenge themselves to make links between the two ideas revealed. This process can be repeated as many times as is purposeful and can be extended by increasing the number of ideas they are seeking to make connections between.

■ An alternative approach is to use a learning matrix. To work through the prestructural and unistructural levels, learners create a grid featuring all the core ideas/ terminology/facts that are integral to the topic they are learning about. To stretch themselves to multistructural and relational thinking, they choose coordinates at random to explore how these ideas link to the wider topic. As with the recall cards, challenge can be increased as learners extend their thinking to considering how pairs or even clusters of three or four coordinates can work together within the context of the topic.

REINTERPRETING NEW IDEAS AND INTEGRATING THEM INTO WHAT YOU KNOW

■ Using the 'pass it on' principle is one way that learners can consolidate what they already know or have learned about a topic, and begin to make more challenging connections between these ideas and new ones. As a baseline task, learners work as a small group to write down all the facts/ideas/principles they already know about the current topic. Once sufficient time has been provided for learners to exhaust their baseline knowledge, they then exchange their ideas sheet with another group. Simple analysis of the new set of ideas can be done. Which ideas are different to the ones they recorded on their sheet? Are learners unfamiliar/unclear about any of the ideas shared? Has this new set of ideas got any clear gaps? The group should add/question/annotate the new set of ideas according to their findings.

When learners are ready for an additional challenge, they can begin examining the ideas presented for links/connections/themes that begin to knit them together.

The sheets can be passed between groups as many times as is purposeful, with different, or perhaps extended, connections emerging with each pass. The swapping need not happen immediately. It may be useful to have learners record the baseline of facts and ideas and not begin to compare/spot differences/make connections until later in the lesson, or perhaps not even until the following lesson, once further input and knowledge have been gained. Colour-coding responses at the different phases of the activity can be a good way to highlight the progress and development of ideas.

ANDY HARGREAVES is the Thomas More Brennan chair at the Lynch School of Education and professor in the Carroll School of Management at Boston College, where he received the 2015 Excellence in Teaching with Technology Award. Previously, he was the co-founder and director of the International Centre for Educational Change at the Ontario Institute for Studies in Education.

Andy has authored or edited over thirty books, several of which have achieved outstanding writing awards in the United States. *Professional Capital: Transforming Teaching in Every School* (with Michael Fullan, 2012) has received three prizes, including the prestigious Grawemeyer Award in Education for 2015. His other recent books include *The Global Fourth Way* (with Dennis Shirley, 2012) and *Uplifting Leadership* (with Alan Boyle and Alma Harris, 2014).

Andy consults with organisations and governments all over the world. He serves as adviser in education to the Premier of Ontario, is the founding editor of two scholarly journals and is president elect of the International Congress for School Effectiveness and Improvement. He holds an honorary doctorate from the University of Uppsala in Sweden and is a Fellow of the Royal Society of Arts in the UK.

CHAPTER 17

UPLIFTING COLLEAGUES

ANDY HARGREAVES

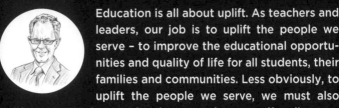

Education is all about uplift. As teachers and leaders, our job is to uplift the people we serve – to improve the educational opportunities and quality of life for all students, their families and communities. Less obviously, to uplift the people we serve, we must also uplift or inspire the people who serve them – staff, colleagues and all the adults in and around the school. One mistake is to try to uplift our students by browbeating the adults to do better or work harder in ways that get them down, put them down or wear them out. The other mistake is to focus so much on uplifting the adults that we forget about the students.

The best strategy is to uplift each other. We should push and pull each other up to learn more, do better, try something else. To uplift each other, we must care about and support each other as people and not just as colleagues. We must be willing to give and ask for help. We must work with school neighbours, even competitors, for the communities we share in common. We must help people to feel proud of the best of their past, yet also strive for a greater future. We must be ready to alert colleagues to when they might be losing their edge or going astray, for the sake of their students and also themselves. In uplifting others, we will then find that we will also uplift ourselves, and in that way be up for the next opportunity or the next challenge.

FURTHER READING

Hargreaves, Andy, Boyle, Alan and Harris, Alma (2014). *Uplifting Leadership: How Organizations, Teams, and Communities Raise Performance* (San Francisco, CA: Jossey-Bass).

Hargreaves, Andy and Fullan, Michael (2012). *Professional Capital: Transforming Teaching in Every School* (New York: Teachers College Press and London: Routledge).

PRACTICAL STRATEGIES

START AN 'UPLIFTING' DIALOGUE

Professionally 'uplifting' our colleagues in ways that also benefit students is not always natural to the way we interact with each other in schools. In a busy and sometimes overwhelming environment, work-related dialogue can be easily consumed by completing administrative tasks or venting frustrations to a friendly and empathetic ear. It is not enough to hope or wish to uplift our colleagues, off the cuff, when there is time left over for it. We need to be deliberate about how we support, reassure, praise, build confidence, compliment and recognise effort and success in our colleagues.

Try the following as ways to bring uplift into the fabric and norm of your school:

- Encourage public 'shout outs'. Ask any Teacher of the Year what the consequence of their elevation was and many will say that colleagues ignored their accomplishments and sometimes even stopped talking to them. Most teachers believe they work hard and deserve recognition. They find it hard to accept why one should be elevated above all of them. Teaching isn't *The X Factor* where only one person wins. This is a problem with the system, not the teachers. With teachers, as with kids, it is important to recognise many examples of success and many individuals who have accomplished things. Start every meeting by recognising two or three successes (not just one and not too many). Vary the individuals and the kinds of successes being recognised. Make them genuine and non-trivial. Model applause and shout-outs for these accomplishments. Post a few a week on the staffroom noticeboard or on the school website, or if you are a large school on an electronic announcements board. Try to tie these back to the school's purpose or improvement effort. If this hasn't been a tradition in your school it may feel uncomfortable at first, but stick with it. And if you are in one of these meetings and someone else gets praised, be the first to start the applause. Effervescence needs someone to be the first bubble. Be effervescent for others as well as for yourself. Humility doesn't mean absence of praise or enthusiasm or quiet self-denial. It means building collective pride by sharing the praise around.

▪ The most delightful moments of uplift are the ones that come intimately, one to one. A handwritten thank-you note for a small kindness a colleague has shown to a child or a parent, for going the extra mile with someone, for having an innovative idea or even for just thinking to bring treats to a meeting – these things can mean all the world to an overworked teacher. Notice when someone is down and say something that will pick them up when you pass them in the hallway – perhaps you have seen something brilliant they were doing in a lesson or have noticed how one child in their class had done something extraordinary. Ask them for an idea or for some input. Tell them when you feel stuck and be monumentally appreciative when they help you get unstuck. It's the quick yet thoughtful ways that make sure our colleagues know the things they do *are* noticed and *are* appreciated which can often make the biggest difference. Do more and more of this (without overdoing it – don't devalue the currency) and see how it spreads. Kindness is contagious!

■ How am I feeling today? Sometimes it is tricky to know who needs uplift the most on your staff team. Creating a display in the staffroom or a place for online interaction where individuals can signal and share with their colleagues how they are feeling professionally can be a good way to get the conversation going. Emojis (emoticons) can be one quick way to do this (though avoid the rude ones!). Don't expect it but do allow it, especially when people may be feeling a bit demoralised. The spectrum of feelings might include really positive states such as 'enthused', 'motivated', 'determined' or 'inspired', but may also include more difficult feelings such as 'perplexed', 'floundering', 'overwhelmed' or 'frustrated'. Once you know how someone is feeling, it will be much easier to have a supportive and uplifting professional conversation with them.

■ Professional learning communities needn't always be endlessly earnest on the one hand or superficially upbeat on the other. Every so often, use a protocol where staff members can talk about a time in the week when they felt a positive emotion about an experience with students, colleagues or parents, what caused it and what was the consequence – and then also do this with a negative or difficult emotion. This can lead to commiseration, compliments, constructive feedback and suggestions – and sometimes just uproarious laughter. Menus of emotions can help here: positive ones might include things like joy, happiness, surprise, pride and satisfaction, and negative ones include frustration, guilt, shame, disgust, anxiety, sadness and anger. But do avoid *Schadenfreude* – taking pleasure in other people's suffering!

CHANNEL THE DIALOGUE THAT DOES NOT 'UPLIFT'

Complaining is cathartic. There is no doubt that when something frustrates you, getting it off your chest in the form of a rant can make you feel a little better. The trouble is that there is no quicker way to turn the collective tone in a negative direction. Bad moods travel fast.

If you need to vent, never do this with or in front of more than one person at a time. Don't embarrass yourself. If you can, try to see the funny side, or even conclude by taking a big sigh and saying, 'Well, I guess I said my piece! I feel 50 pounds lighter now!' This makes you visibly distance yourself from the intensity of your feelings.

If you are witness to someone else venting, try to empathise without escalating things. This needn't be a pious and therapeutic expression of 'I know how you feel'. It can also be a short story of a similar incident that turns tragedy into comedy – at your own expense. Be your own fall guy here. It's hard for people to stay angry when they are cracking up with laughter!

And a few rules for venting on social media or digital platforms: mainly – don't. Put a critical or complaining email into a Word document first and save it for a few hours before sending. The chances are you'll feel better for just writing it and never send it at all. Don't email, tweet or go on other social media when you are tired, annoyed, sick, overworked, in the middle of something or have had a few beers!

Last, try to make sure that in the notes or words you give to your boss there are more positives than negatives. Leaders spend a lot of time listening to people who are complaining or who want things. Spontaneously praising and thanking your boss isn't being a creep! It simply recognises that bosses need to be thanked and praised too. Hardly anyone ever thinks of this. Lift up the people above you as well as the ones below.

AVOID WEARING PEOPLE OUT

■ Time is a teacher's most precious commodity. If we want to introduce a new initiative in our school then formal time should be ring fenced for this to happen. Telling colleagues that a new programme or idea – peer coaching, for example – is key to the school's success, but not allocating official time for the necessary work to take place, sends a very ambiguous message about its true importance. Sometimes it may be necessary to sacrifice more routine aspects of business in order to schedule in time for new developments to take root. If you invest in a bit of time for colleagues to work together, and the work is worthwhile, these colleagues will then often devote even more time of their own. Self-sacrifice and martyrdom is ultimately not uplifting at all.

■ Leave some things be. Not every problem needs an intervention right now. Sometimes, if you leave things alone, people will resolve things for themselves – like a squabble between colleagues. You don't have to be everyone's problem-solver for them. And you don't have to answer all your emails right away. Happiness isn't an empty inbox. Get away from the screen, take a walk, spend some quality time face to face and then come back to your inbox later or on another day. When you empty your inbox, you are filling up someone else's, so think about what really needs to be done now and what can be left until later.

WORKING WITH NEIGHBOURS AND COMPETITORS

■ Make contact with neighbouring schools and suggest sharing best practice. You might set up an electronic platform where teachers can share resources and ideas across establishments in your community, or simply consult nearby schools to establish common development needs so that you can team up to attend to these together. If your fellow educationalists down the road have already invented the wheel, you may as well borrow their pattern and swap it for a ground-breaking invention of your own. Learners benefit when schools work together to pool their best ideas and collaboratively develop them even further; they can be disadvantaged when schools – through a sense of competition – insist on acting in isolation.

■ Exchange or donate staff for a few hours a week to assist in areas where one of you is a bit further ahead than the other. If you lift each other up, you will lift yourselves up in the process.

NEXT STEPS ...

TEACHER DEVELOPMENT TRUST

Progress is fundamental to us as teachers and we want to get better at making it happen for the young people we teach.

We love being teachers because we love seeing pupils learn. Every teacher hopes that they will help pupils progress through school and into adult life as successful and confident individuals. It is a delicious idea that we can grow as a teacher and help more children make more progress next year than we could in this one.

However, as this book has demonstrated, the idea of progress gets more difficult the more you look at it. It is philosophically, scientifically and pedagogically complex, and yet it underpins the work we do in the classroom. Coupled with that, it turns out that teachers' own learning is complex.

We commissioned an international review of the research into what types of training and development (also sometimes known as continuing professional development, CPD or just PD) actually help us to make the most difference (Teacher Development Trust, 2015).

Let's pull these ideas together and identify some key actions that can turn this book into a powerful starting point for development which makes a difference.

GETTING STARTED: PLAN AND ENGAGE

No matter how excited you are about the ideas in this book, the most important thing you need to do is pause and plan. You need a strategy to engage staff in a long-term learning process which is relevant to their needs, aspirations and interests.

The research suggests that you need to design a sustained, *responsive learning* process – that is, *not* one which is about learning and performing a checklist of practices or, conversely, engaging in prolonged pondering of the theory only. Teachers learn best when they pay close attention to the impact they are having on pupils and respond to feedback from the classroom to refine, challenge and build their knowledge and skill. This needs to be weaved together with deep, professional thinking about why and how different approaches are working (or not).

Key elements of this preparation and planning stage include:

■ Finding time: identifying and protecting time when teachers can discuss and collaborate around improving practice.

- Prioritising and accommodating: working with a range of colleagues to identify what tasks would be most useful to take away or postpone in order to make time to engage in learning around progress.

- Expectation raising: sending small groups of staff to other schools who have thought deeply about progress, who are further along the road and who are achieving more with a similar cohort of pupils and in a similar context.

- Leading and selecting: identifying which senior leader(s) will initiate and sustain the programme of learning, which team of internal champions and experts they will work with and how they will negotiate with other leaders in order to find a way to keep the learning about progress coherent with other school policies, plans and procedures.

All of these processes need to be sustained for as long as the teacher learning continues.

CARRYING OUT RESPONSIVE LEARNING

A great way to engage in professional learning is to begin with a pilot which involves an initial group of champions who start the work in the classroom.

Begin by getting group members to collect evidence from classrooms and bring this to a series of regular meetings. Assemble pieces of class work, tests and homework from across a term or over time. Ask group members to pick a topic and record short (audio or video) clips of discussions with pupils, asking them about their thinking about the topic using concrete examples of questions, tasks or problems. Repeat this over the next few lessons and probe how learners' confidence and understanding appears to change. Go into each other's classrooms and focus on two or three pupils as they engage in the learning. Observe how they interact with other pupils and the teacher – how what they say, watch, hear and do affects their progress.

In parallel, carry out a regular reading task between the discussion meetings. For example, ask colleagues to read each chapter in this book and bring their reflections on how it gives a new perspective. In group discussions, tease out where the author's thinking differs from others, what evidence it is based upon and how it fits or contrasts with other chapters. The aims at this stage are to:

- Encourage colleagues to start considering very different views and perspectives.

- Become aware of a variety of opinions and critically assess the evidence base of each.

- Use each author's lens to view current school practice and try to understand the significance of the evidence that the group is collecting.

Identify the most promising ideas that arise from each discussion. Park these on a 'strategies' document and consider which are the most plausible, evidence based and most likely to be effective.

Finally, in each meeting identify what you need to find out more about, diagnose and uncover within group members' classrooms. Each person should choose a strategy and ideally stick with it for a few iterations of improvement. This needs to be accompanied by a clear sense of what should change in the evidence that is being collected – for example, how will essays, answers, interviews and/or observations differ if the strategy is working?

Once your pilot group has worked through the key ideas, you can share these with other staff through displays, short Teach-Meet-style presentations and marketplace or 'speed-dating' events where other staff move around different presentations and ask questions. This can act as a spark for a second, wider round of work as you extend the thinking to a larger portion of staff.

CONNECT AND SHARE

Both research and practical experience suggest that effective CPD needs an external facilitator to make it really effective. This book is a powerful starting point to get some different perspectives. However, you don't want this stimulus to be a flash in the pan. To ensure that the ideas are properly explored and embedded, you need to consider how you can work with one or more experts in the area.

Most of the contributors in this book are on Twitter and many have their own blogs. It may be worth contacting some of them to share your ideas and explore ways to work together. You could find out whether they are speaking at conferences near you and prepare some questions, or you could try to get them to come and speak – perhaps via Skype or as a shared endeavour among a group of schools.

Another option is to find out about leading practitioners and academics in your area. Many universities will have academics who have studied assessment, pedagogy and learning – you could contact their education departments and/or psychology departments.

You could also engage with subject associations and specialist assessment organisations. This works just as well at primary level, where most teachers are generalists, as it helps to connect them with rich subject-based expertise – something that the research suggests is central to high quality teacher development.

Experts can play a number of highly important roles. If possible, ask them to:

- Explore the evidence that you're collecting from your classrooms.

- Suggest ways of collecting even better evidence.

- Signpost further reading and examples of schools to look into.

- Model/demonstrate alternative approaches.

- Act as coaches and discussion facilitators.

FURTHER READING

Coe, Robert, Aloisi, Cesare, Higgins, Steve and Elliot Major, Lee (2014). *What Makes Great Teaching: Review of the Underpinning Research* (London: Sutton Trust). Available at: http://www.sutton-trust.com/researcharchive/great-teaching/.

Teacher Development Trust (2015). *Developing Great Teaching: Lessons from the International Reviews Into Effective Professional Development* (London: TDT). Available at: http://TDTrust.org/about/dgt.

Timperley, Helen, Wilson, Aaron, Barrar, Heather and Fung, Irene (2007). *The Teacher Professional Learning and Development: Best Evidence Synthesis Iteration (BES)* (Wellington: Ministry of Education). Available at: https://www.educationcounts.govt.nz/publications/series/2515/15341.